Collins

11+
Non-Verbal Reasoning

Quick Practice Tests
Ages 10-11

Faisal Nasim

Contents

ACKNOWLEDGEMENTS

The author and publisher are grateful to the copyright holders for permission to use quoted materials and images.

All images are © HarperCollins*Publishers* Limited.

Every effort has been made to trace copyright holders and obtain their permission for the use of copyright material. The author and publisher will gladly receive information enabling them to rectify any error or omission in subsequent editions. All facts are correct at time of going to press.

Published by Collins

An imprint of HarperCollins*Publishers* Limited

1 London Bridge Street
London SE1 9GF

ISBN: 9781844198955

First published 2017
This edition published 2020
Previously published as Letts

10 9 8 7

© HarperCollins*Publishers* Limited 2020

All rights reserved. No part of this publication may be reproduced, stored in a retrieval system, or transmitted, in any form or by any means, electronic, mechanical, photocopying, recording or otherwise, without the prior permission of Collins.

1st Floor, Watermarque Building, Ringsend Road
Dublin 4, Ireland

British Library Cataloguing in Publication Data.

A CIP record of this book is available from the British Library.

Author: Faisal Nasim

Commissioning Editor: Michelle I'Anson

Editor and Project Manager: Sonia Dawkins

Cover Design: Kevin Robbins and Sarah Duxbury

Text Design, Layout and Artwork: Q2A Media

Production: Paul Harding

Printed by RRD South China

Printed and bound in the UK using 100% Renewable Electricity at CPI Group (UK) Ltd

MIX
Paper from
responsible sources
FSC
www.fsc.org   FSC™ C007454

Please note that Collins is not associated with CEM in any way. This book does not contain any official questions and it is not endorsed by CEM.

Our question types are based on those set by CEM, but we cannot guarantee that your child's actual 11+ exam will contain the same question types or format as this book.

About this book

Familiarisation with 11+ test-style questions is a critical step in preparing your child for the 11+ selection tests. This book gives children lots of opportunities to test themselves in short, manageable bursts, helping to build confidence and improve the chance of test success.

It contains 25 tests designed to build key non-verbal reasoning skills.

- Each test is designed to be completed within a short amount of time. Frequent, short bursts of revision are found to be more productive than lengthier sessions.

- CEM tests often consist of a series of shorter, time-pressured sections so these practice tests will help your child become accustomed to this style of questioning.

- If your child does not complete any of the tests in the allocated time, they may need further practice in that area.

- We recommend your child uses a pencil to complete the tests, so that they can rub out the answers and try again at a later date if necessary.

- Children will need a pencil and a rubber to complete the tests and some spare paper for rough working. They will also need to be able to see a clock/watch and should have a quiet place in which to do the tests.

- Answers to every question are provided at the back of the book, with explanations given where appropriate.

- After completing the tests, children should revisit their weaker areas and attempt to improve their scores and timings for those tests.

Download a free progress chart from our website
collins.co.uk/11plus

Test 1

You have 5 minutes to complete this test.

You have 10 questions to complete within the given time.

In each question, there are figures arranged in a large square.

One figure is missing and its place is shown by a question mark.

Circle the letter below the answer choice that should replace the question mark.

EXAMPLE

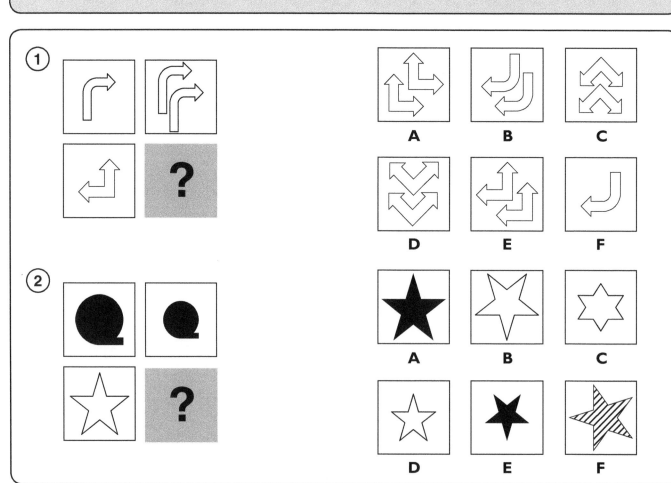

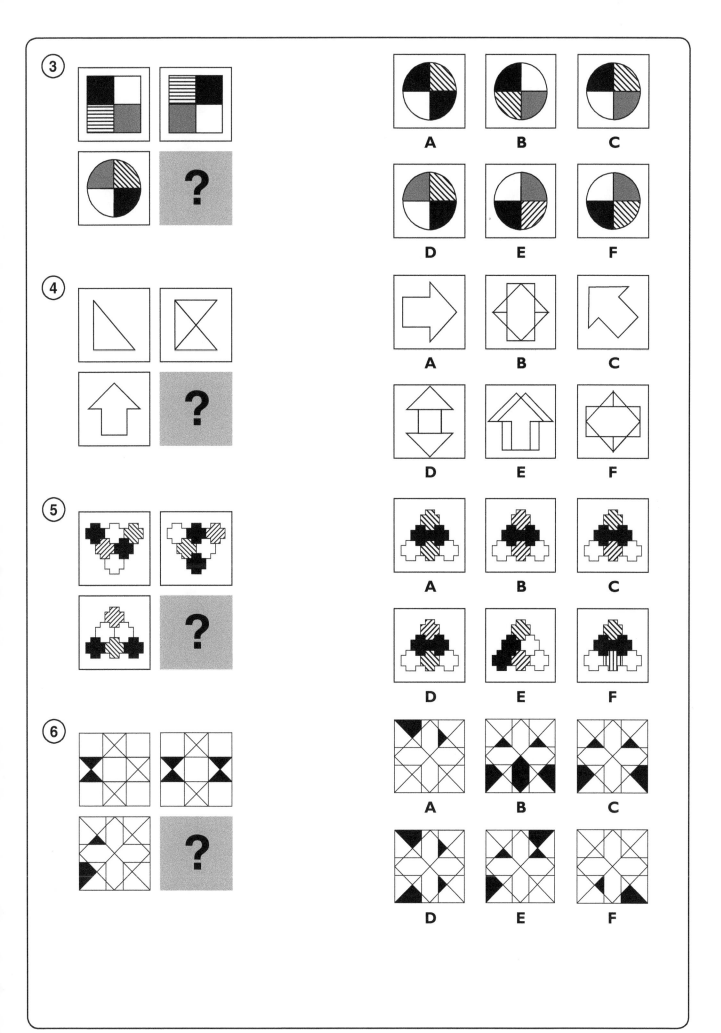

Questions continue on next page

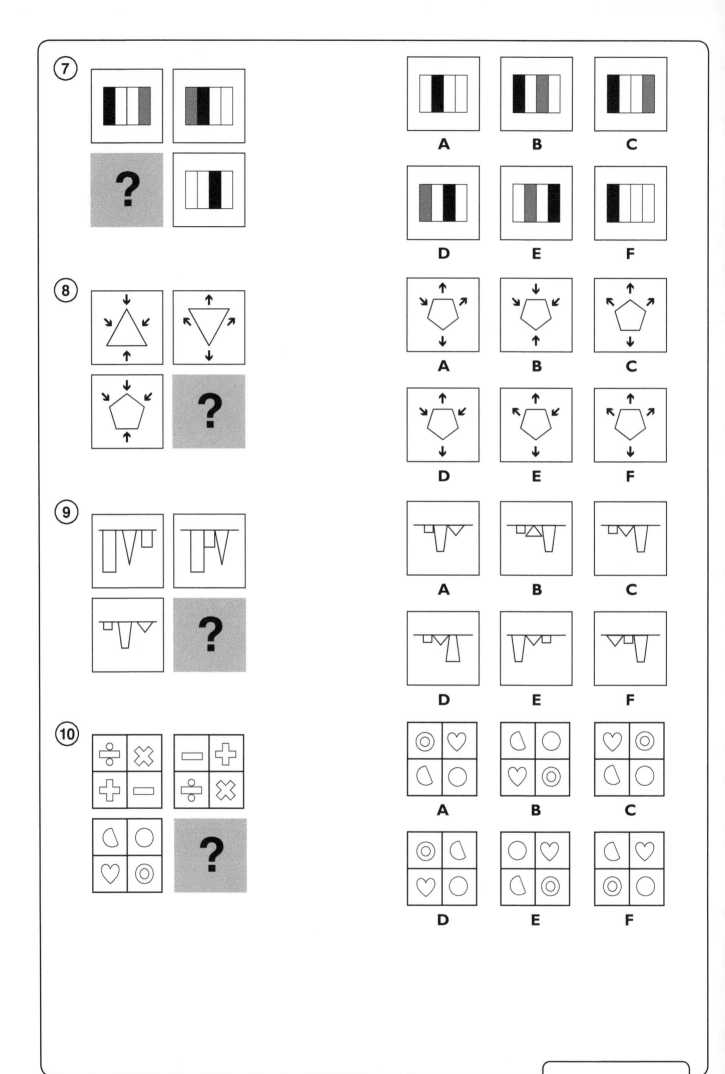

Test 2

Circle the letters below the two figures that show the same shape or pattern.

EXAMPLE

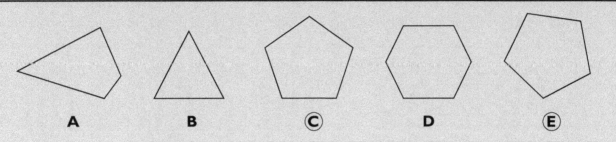

A   B   Ⓒ   D   Ⓔ

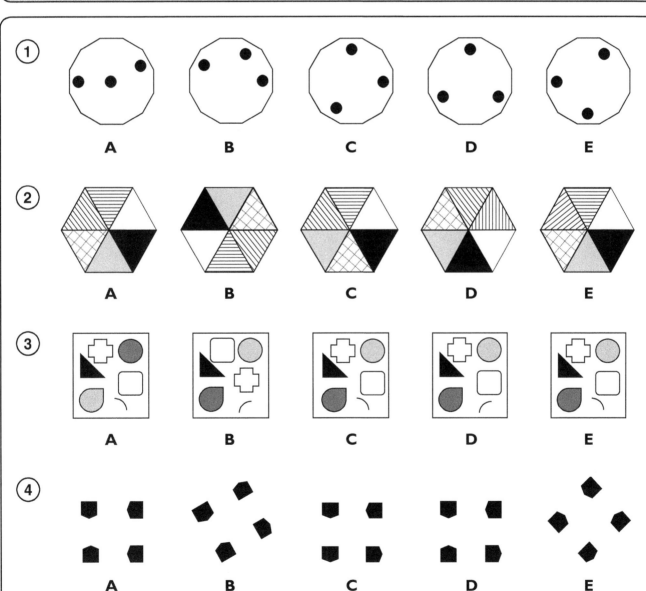

Questions continue on next page

7

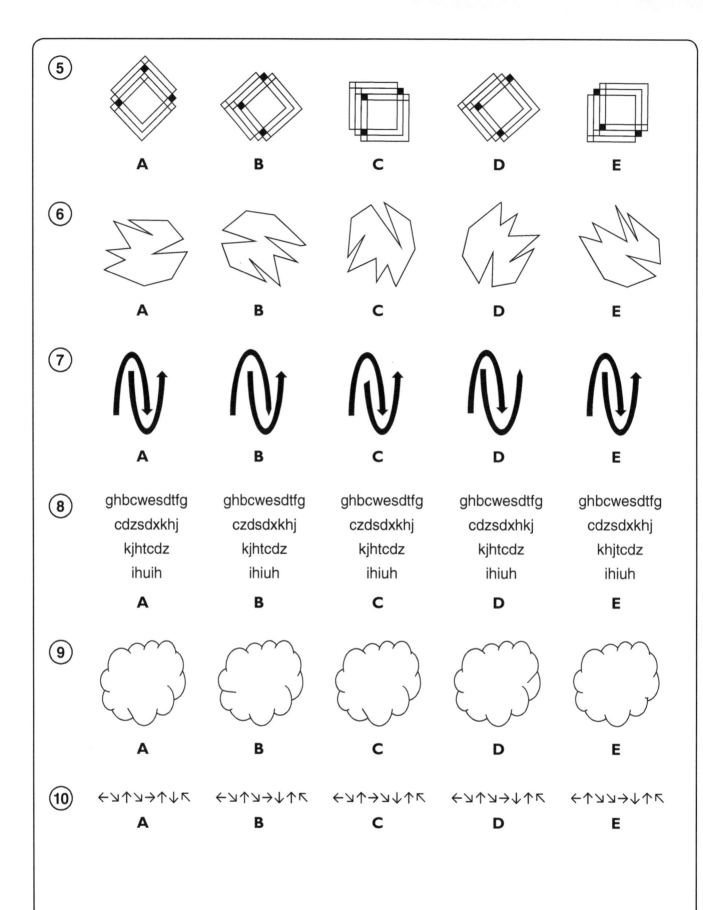

5   A   B   C   D   E

6   A   B   C   D   E

7   A   B   C   D   E

8
ghbcwesdtfg   ghbcwesdtfg   ghbcwesdtfg   ghbcwesdtfg   ghbcwesdtfg
cdzsdxkhj   czdsdxkhj   czdsdxkhj   cdzsdxhkj   cdzsdxkhj
kjhtcdz   kjhtcdz   kjhtcdz   kjhtcdz   khjtcdz
ihuih   ihiuh   ihiuh   ihiuh   ihiuh
A   B   C   D   E

9   A   B   C   D   E

10   ←↘↑↘→↑↓↖   ←↘↑↘→↓↑↖   ←↓↑→↘↓↑↖   ←↘↑↘→↓↑↖   ←↑↘↘→↓↑↖
     A   B   C   D   E

Score: .... / 10

Test 3

You have 5 minutes to complete this test.

You have 10 questions to complete within the given time.

The three figures on the left are similar in some way.

Work out how they are similar and then circle the letter below the figure from the answer choices that goes with them.

EXAMPLE

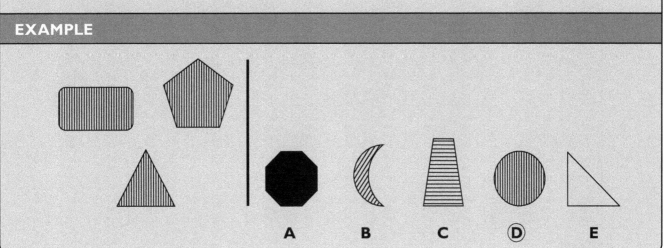

A   B   C   D   E

①

②

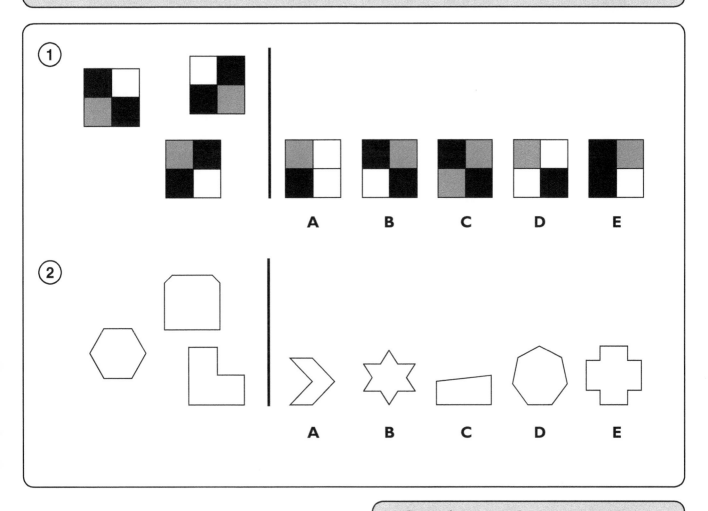

Questions continue on next page

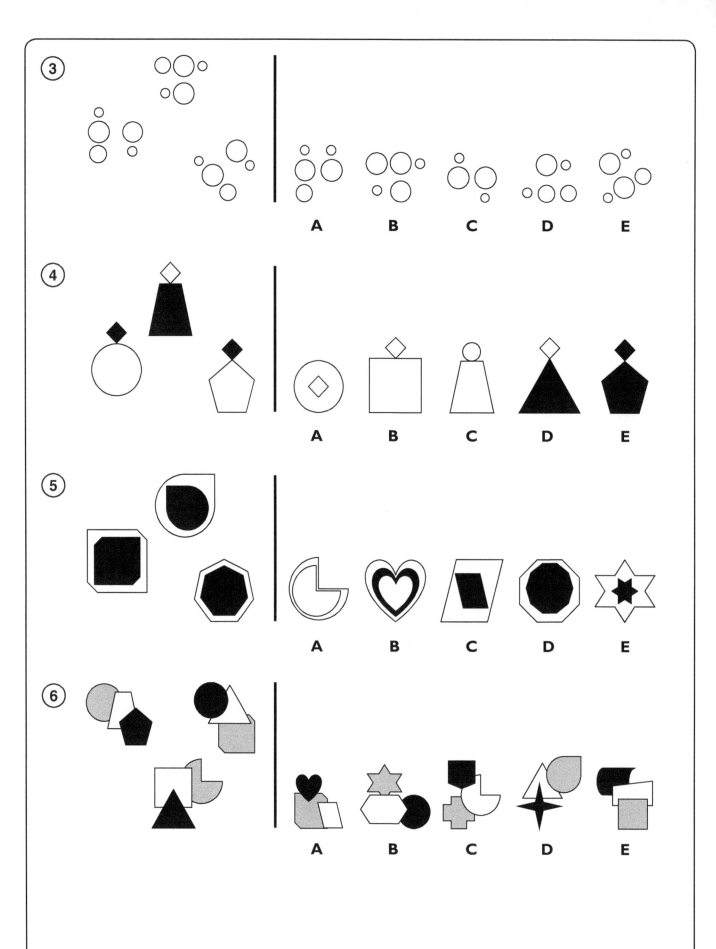

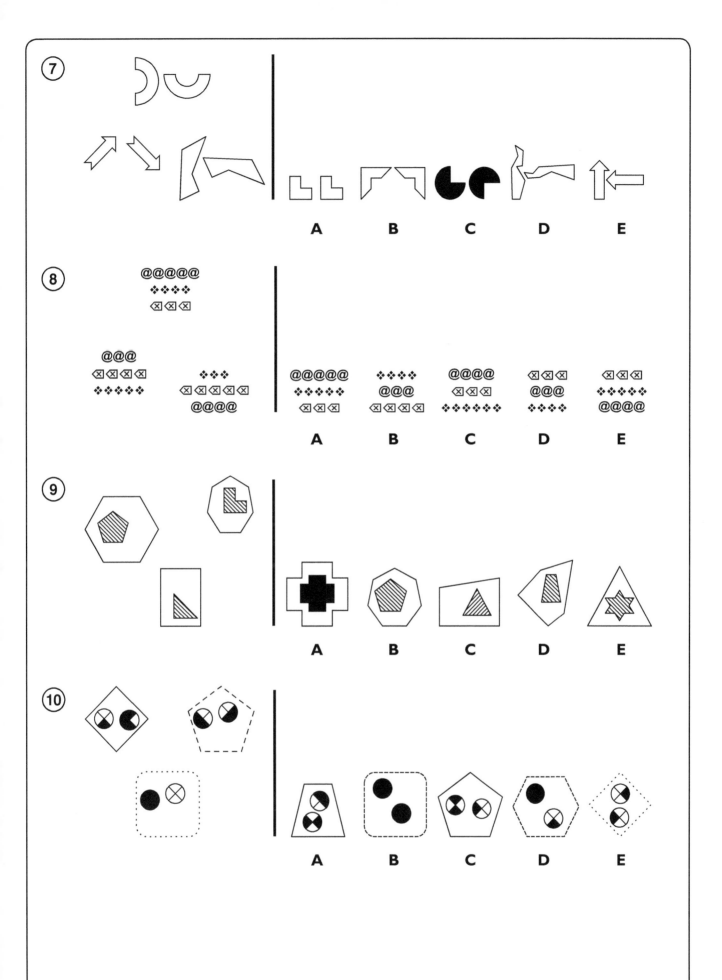

Test 4

You have 5 minutes to complete this test.

You have 10 questions to complete within the given time.

The 'net' on the left is folded to make the cube shown.

One of the faces of the cube has been left blank.

Circle the letter below the figure on the right that should occupy the blank face of the cube.

EXAMPLE

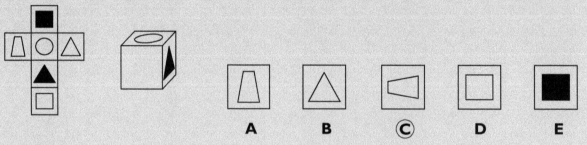

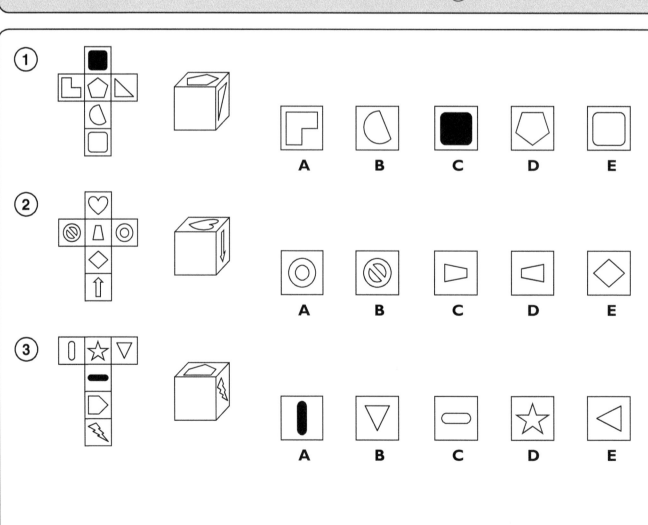

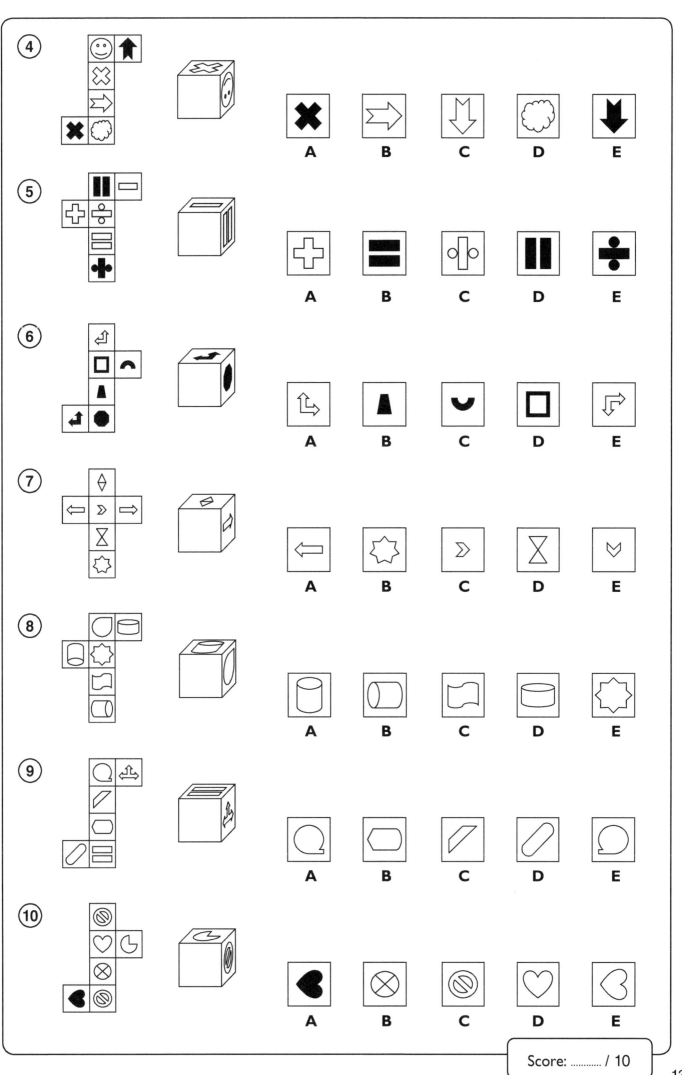

Test 5

You have 5 minutes to complete this test.

You have 10 questions to complete within the given time.

Circle the letter below the figure on the right that shows the top-down, plan view of the 3D figure on the left.

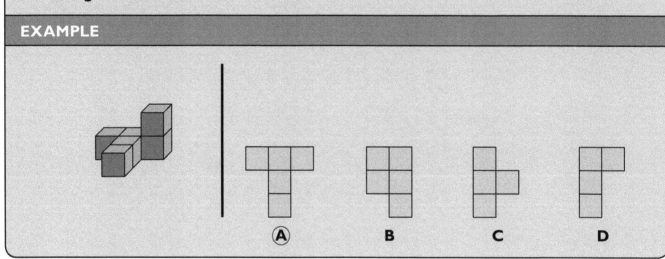

A   B   C   D

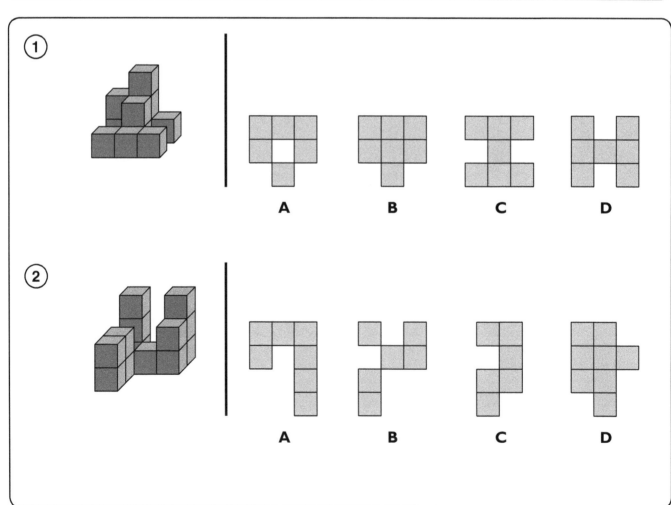

①

A   B   C   D

②

A   B   C   D

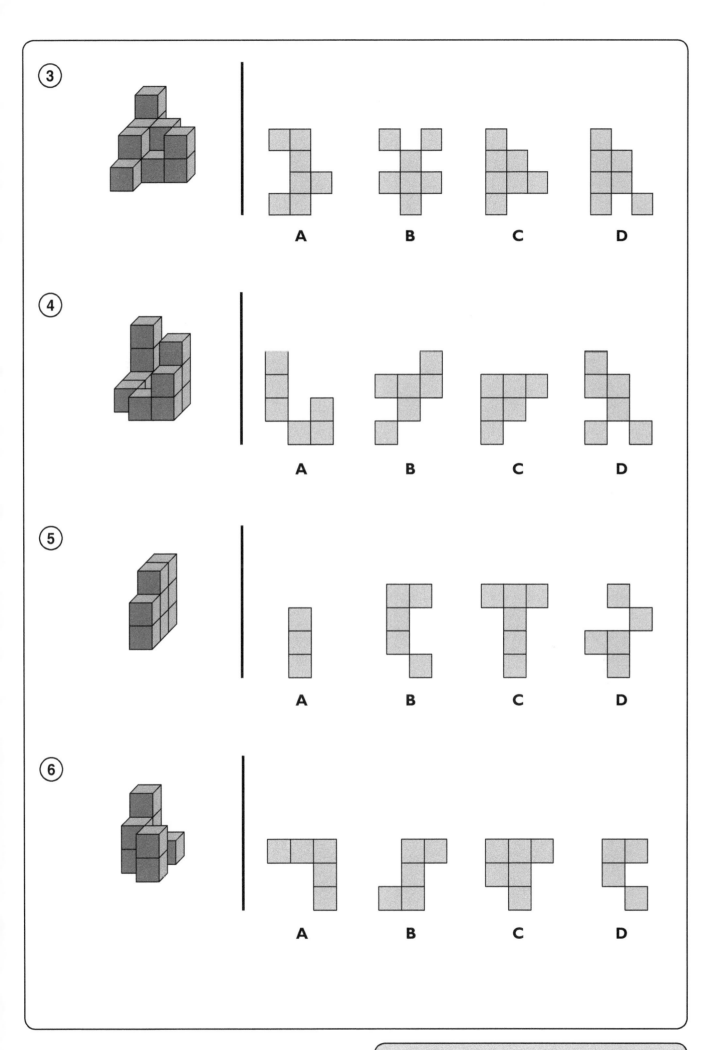

Questions continue on next page

15

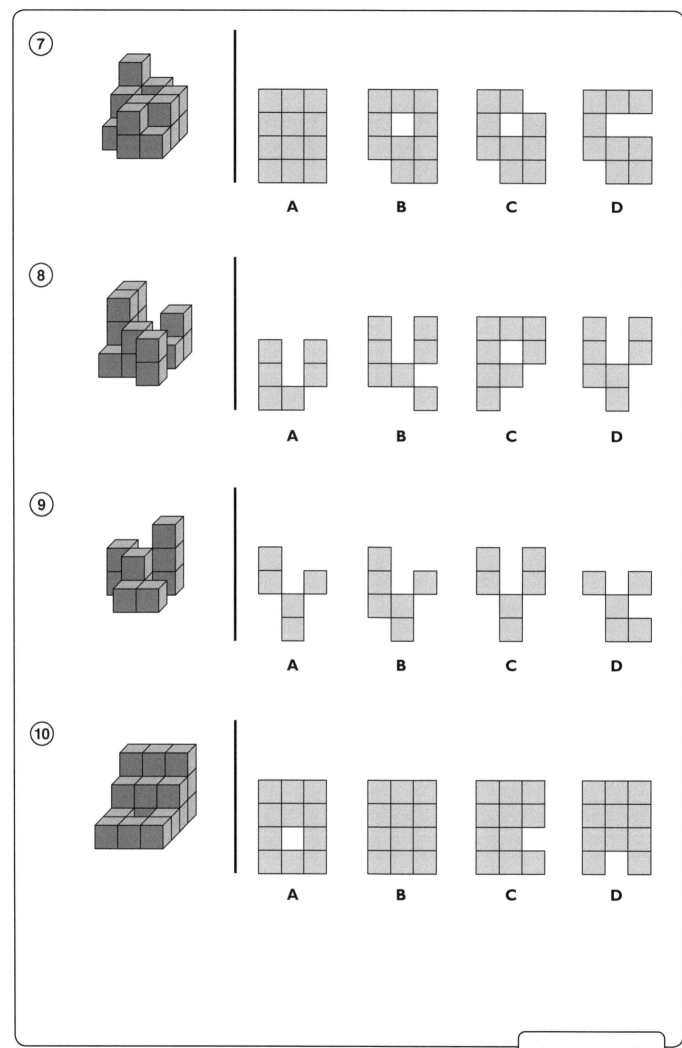

⑦

A B C D

⑧

A B C D

⑨

A B C D

⑩

A B C D

Score: .... / 10

16

Test 6

You have 5 minutes to complete this test.

You have 10 questions to complete within the given time.

Circle the letter below the figure on the right that looks like the figure on the left when it is reflected over the line.

EXAMPLE

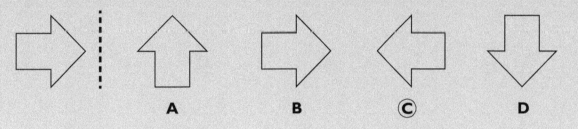

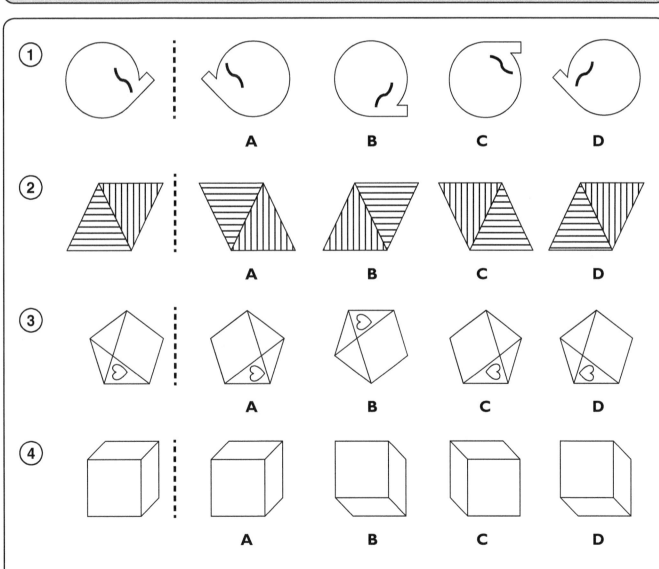

Questions continue on next page

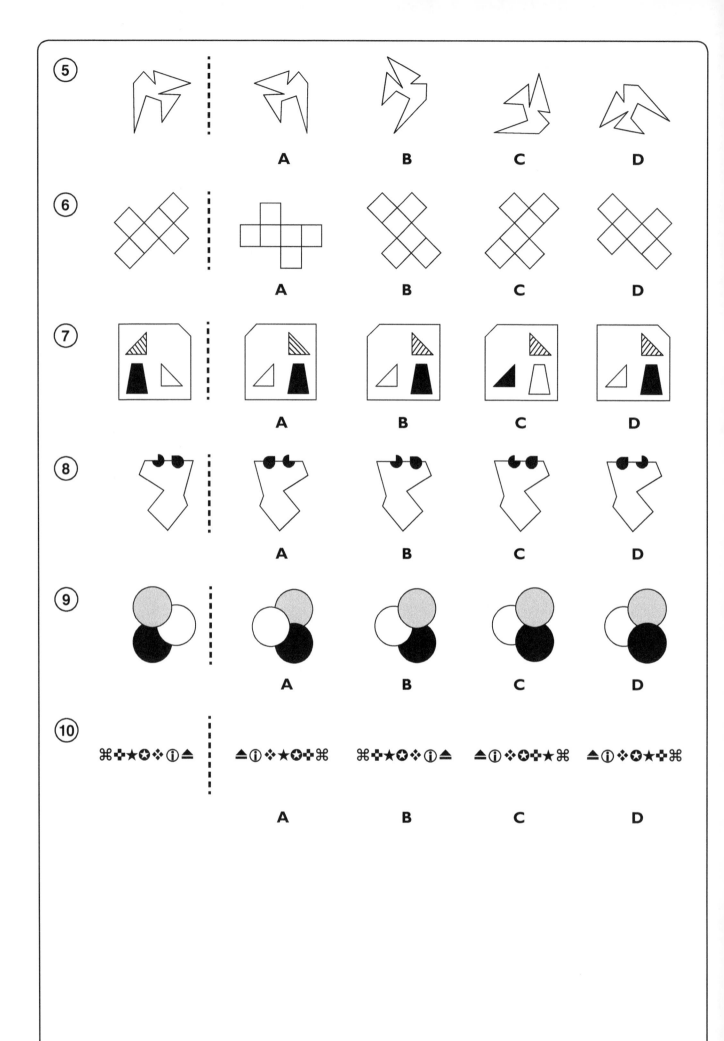

5   A   B   C   D

6   A   B   C   D

7   A   B   C   D

8   A   B   C   D

9   A   B   C   D

10   A   B   C   D

Score: .... / 10

Test 7

You have 5 minutes to complete this test.

You have 10 questions to complete within the given time.

In each question there is a sequence of patterned squares with one missing.

Circle the letter below the square that shows the missing pattern.

EXAMPLE

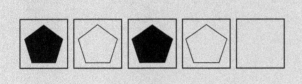

Ⓐ   B   C

D   E   F

---

①

      A B C

A   B   C

D   E   F

②

A   B   C

D   E   F

Questions continue on next page

19

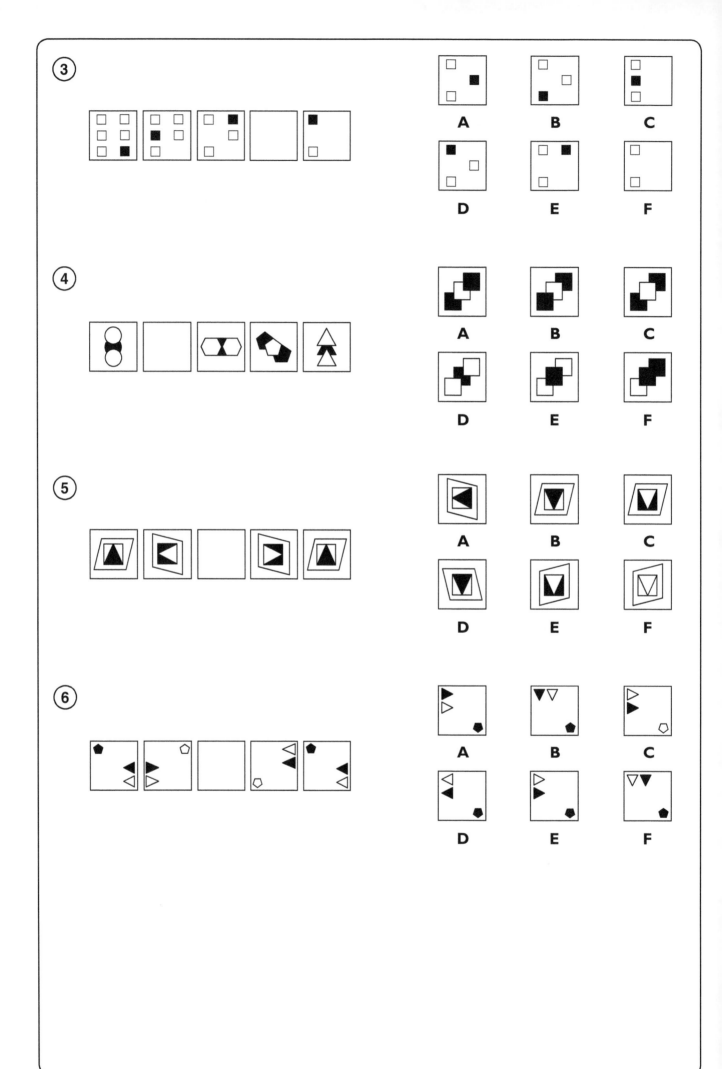

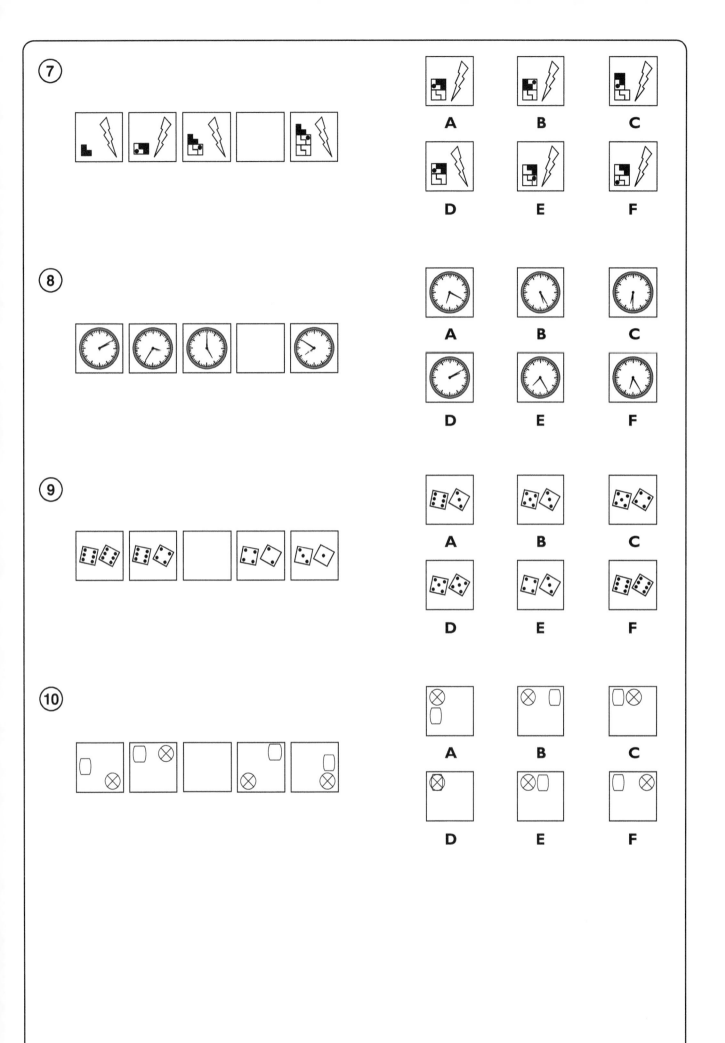

Test 8

You have 5 minutes to complete this test.

You have 10 questions to complete within the given time.

Each figure on the left has a code next to it. The code consists of letters. The figure on the right has no code next to it.

Circle the letter below the code on the right that best describes the figure on the right.

EXAMPLE

	AZ
	AY
	BZ

	AZ	BZ	AX	CZ	BY
	A	**B**	**C**	**D**	**(E)**

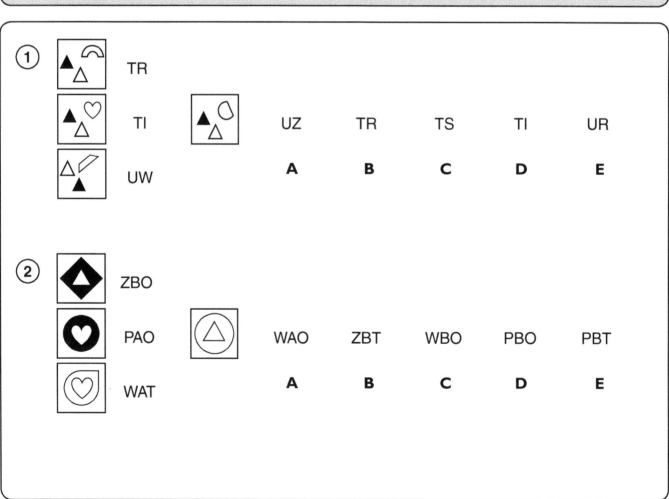

1

	TR
	TI
	UW

	UZ	TR	TS	TI	UR
	A	**B**	**C**	**D**	**E**

2

	ZBO
	PAO
	WAT

	WAO	ZBT	WBO	PBO	PBT
	A	**B**	**C**	**D**	**E**

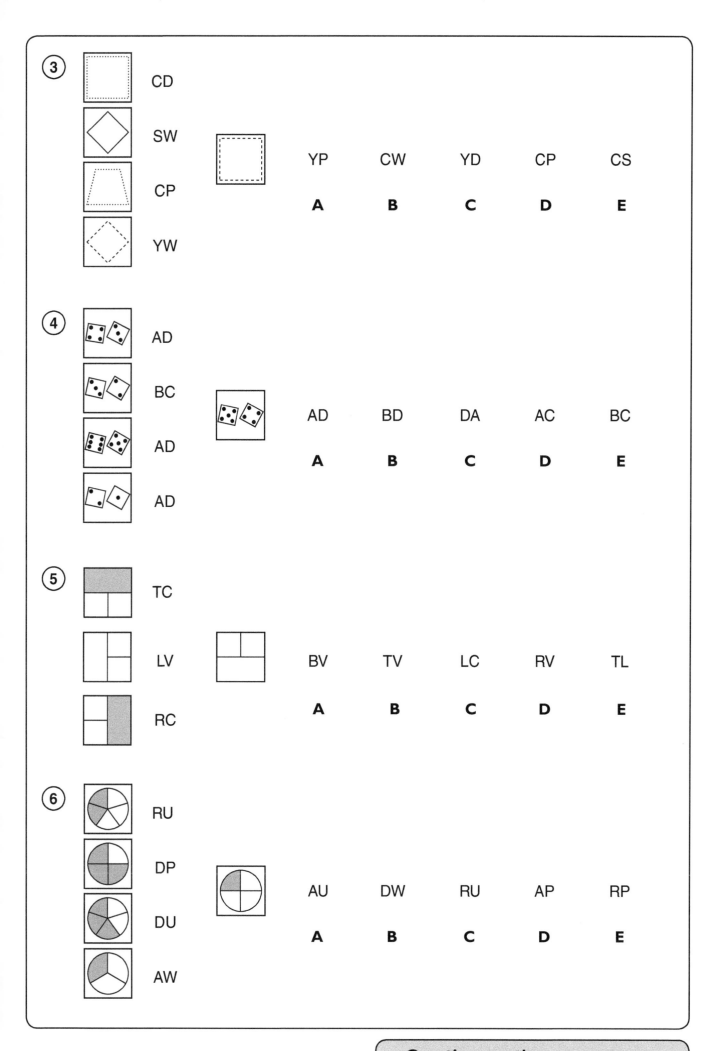

Questions continue on next page

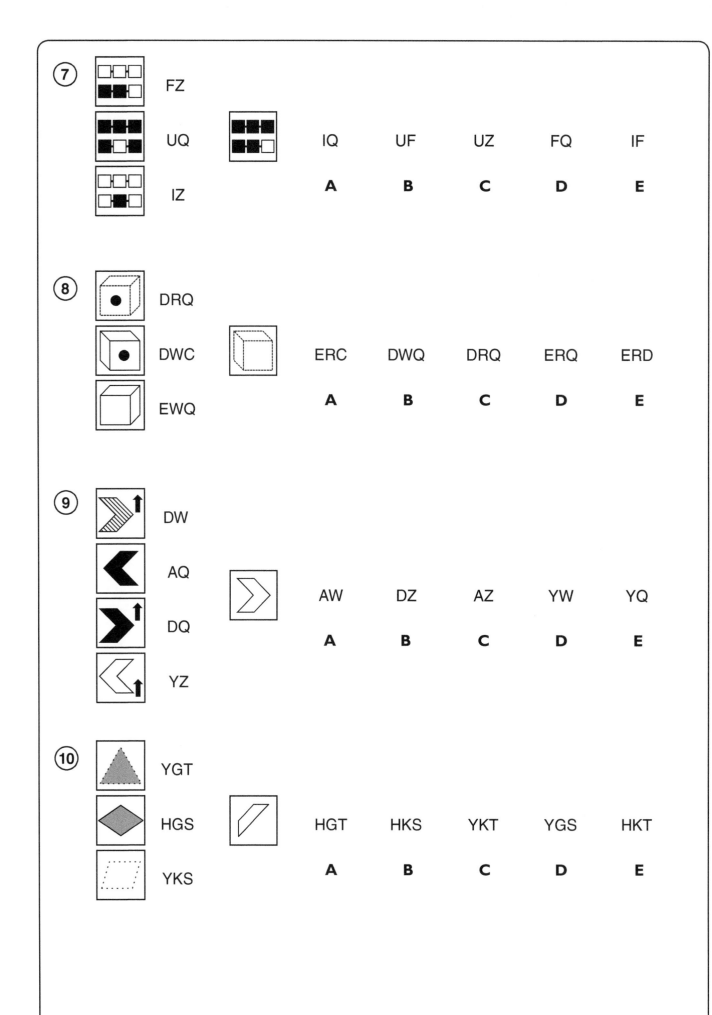

⑦ FZ UQ IZ

IQ UF UZ FQ IF
A   B   C   D   E

⑧ DRQ DWC EWQ

ERC DWQ DRQ ERQ ERD
A   B   C   D   E

⑨ DW AQ DQ YZ

AW DZ AZ YW YQ
A   B   C   D   E

⑩ YGT HGS YKS

HGT HKS YKT YGS HKT
A   B   C   D   E

Score: .... / 10

24

Test 9

You have 5 minutes to complete this test.

You have 10 questions to complete within the given time.

There are two figures on the left with an arrow between them. Decide how the second is related to the first.

There is a third figure followed by an arrow and four more figures.

Circle the letter below the figure that is related to the third figure in the same way that the first two figures are related to each other.

EXAMPLE

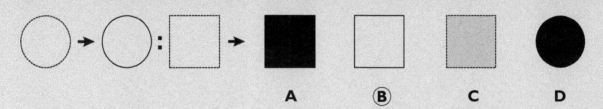

A	Ⓑ	C	D

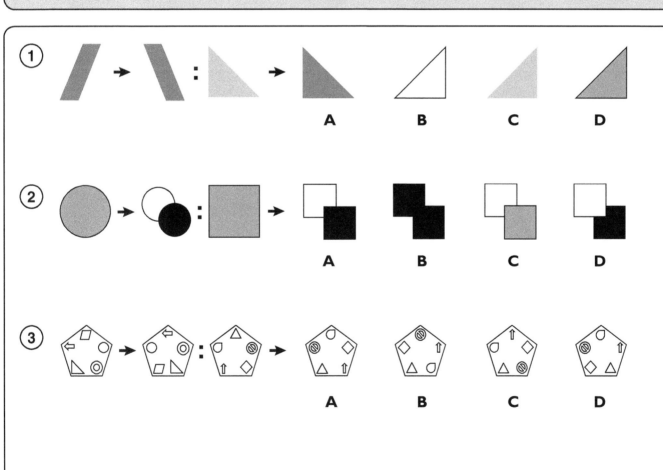

Questions continue on next page

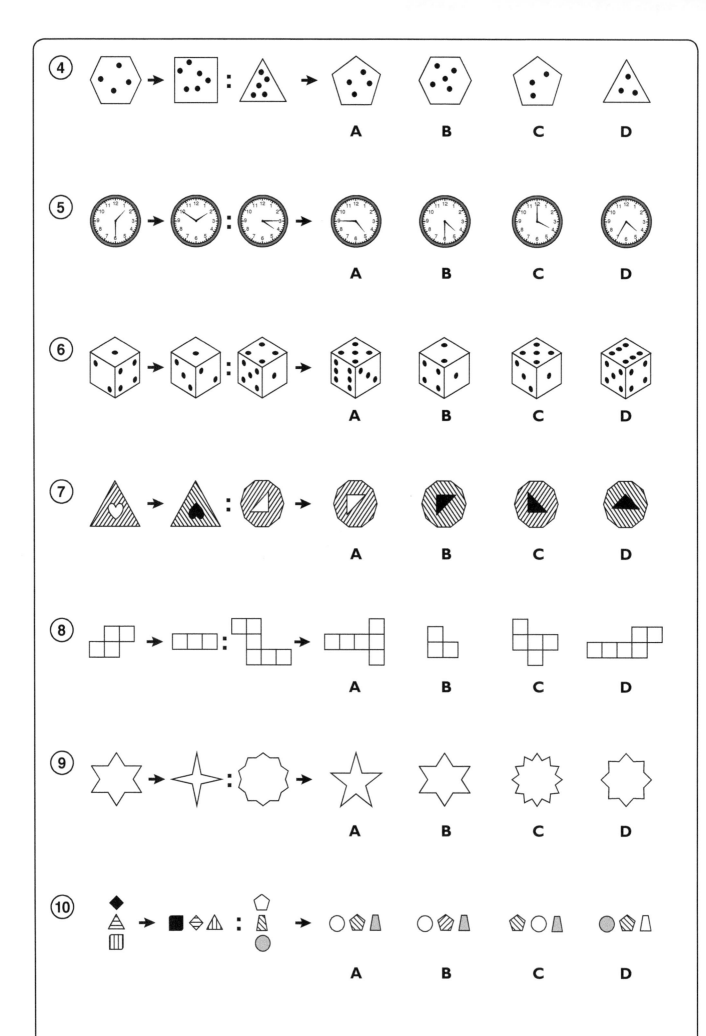

④

⑤

⑥

⑦

⑧

⑨

⑩

A   B   C   D

Test 10

You have 5 minutes to complete this test.

You have 10 questions to complete within the given time.

Circle the letter below the figure that is most unlike the others.

EXAMPLE

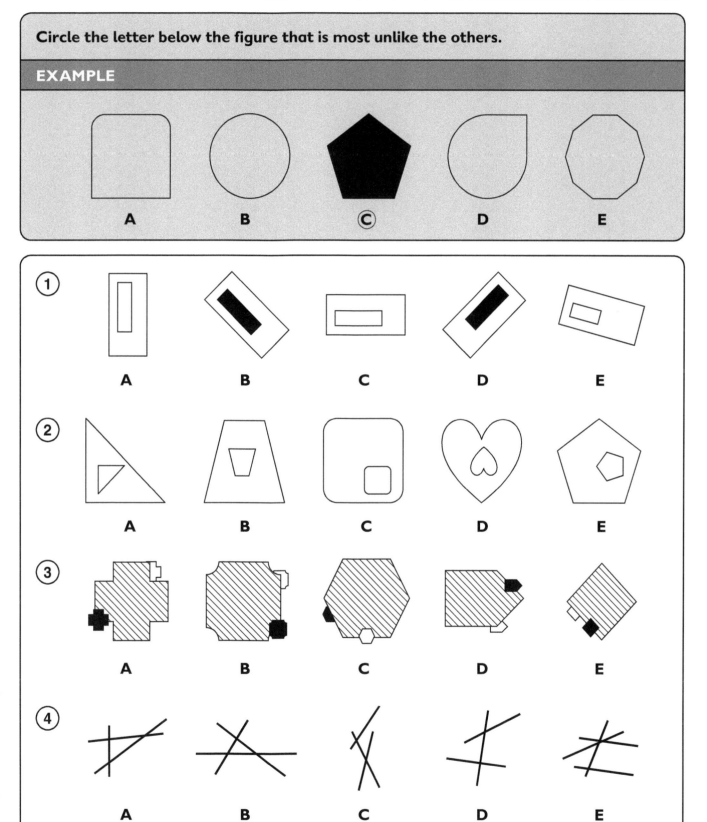

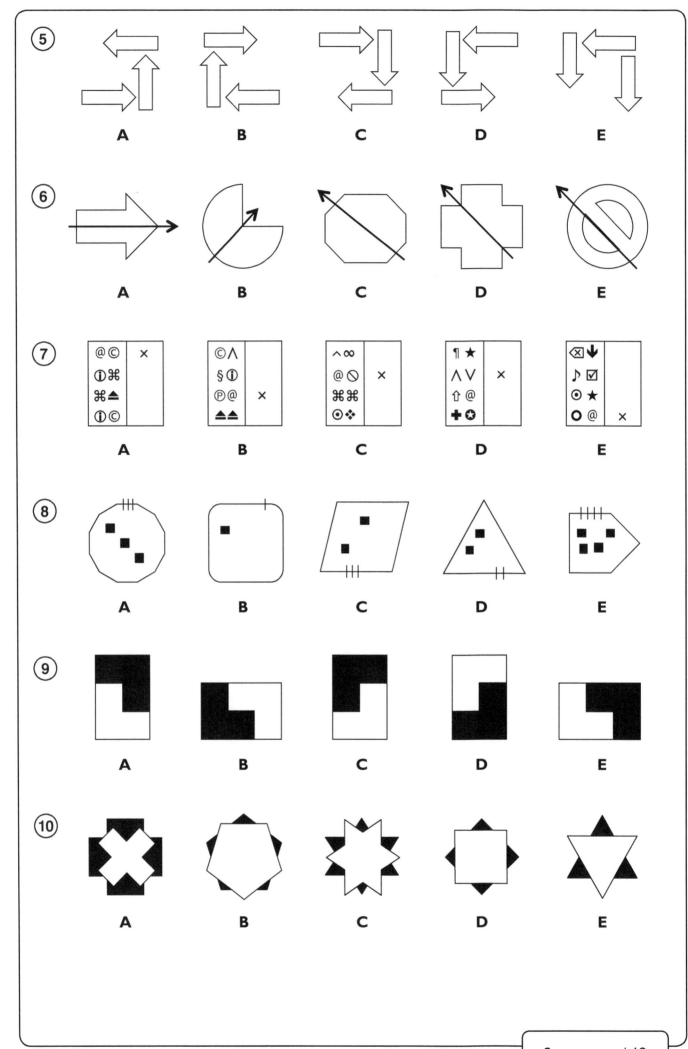

Score: .... / 10

Test 11

You have 5 minutes to complete this test.

You have 10 questions to complete within the given time.

In each question, there are figures arranged in a large square.

One figure is missing and its place is shown by a question mark.

Circle the letter below the answer choice that should replace the question mark.

EXAMPLE

1

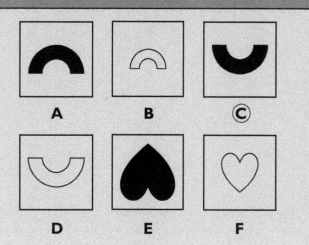

2

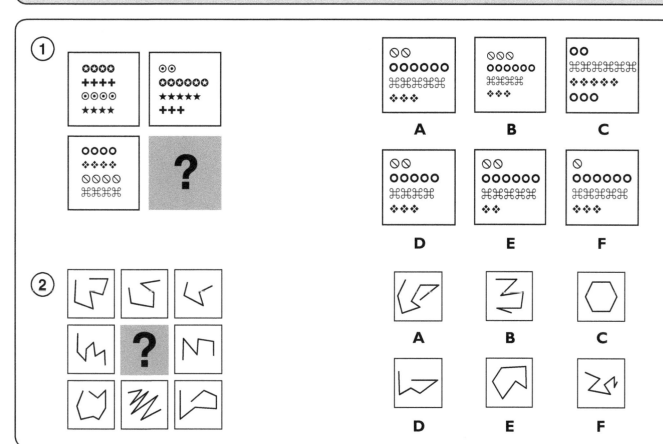

Questions continue on next page

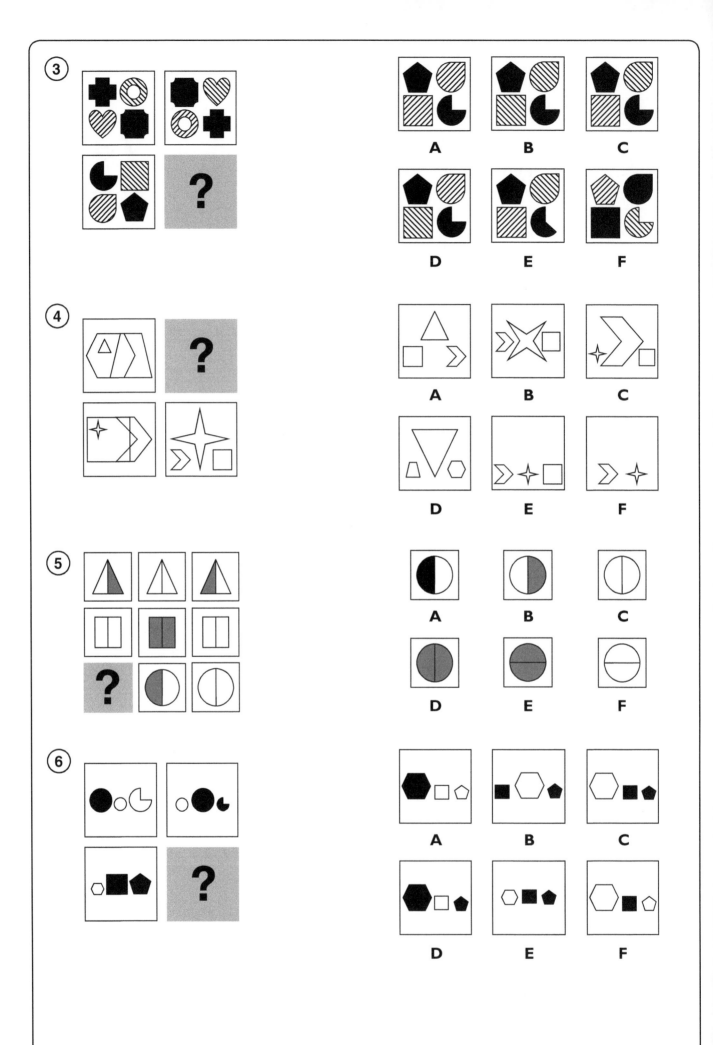

3

4

5

6

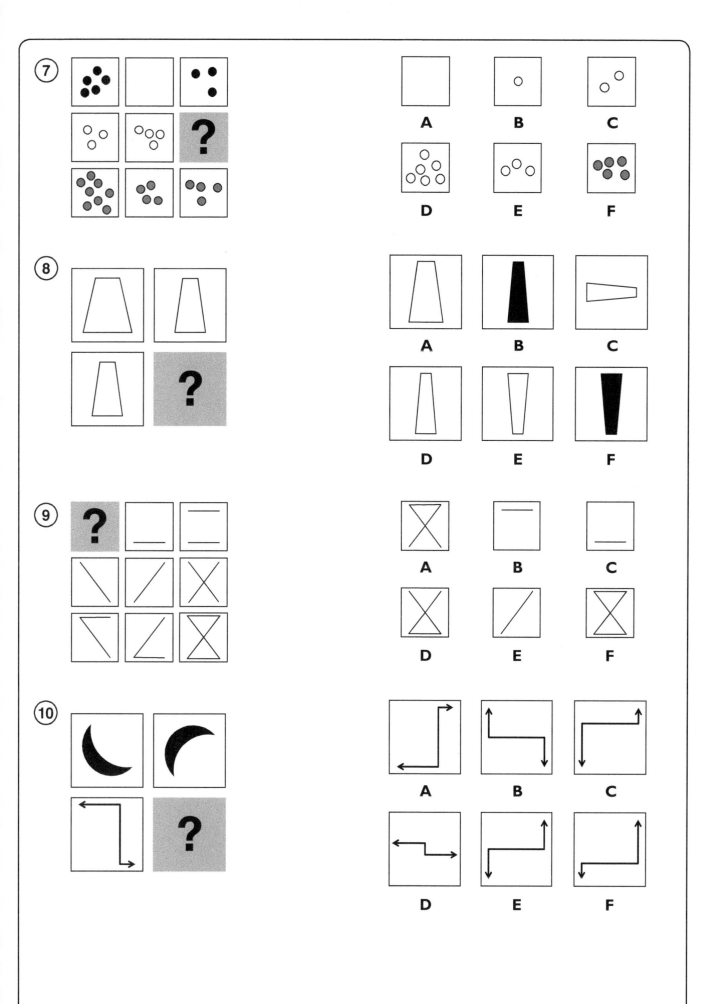

Test 12

You have 5 minutes to complete this test.

You have 10 questions to complete within the given time.

Circle the letters below the two figures that show the same shape or pattern.

EXAMPLE

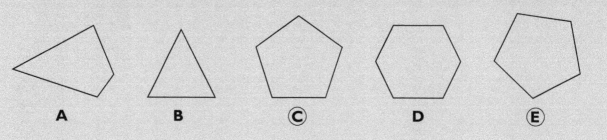

A   B   Ⓒ   D   Ⓔ

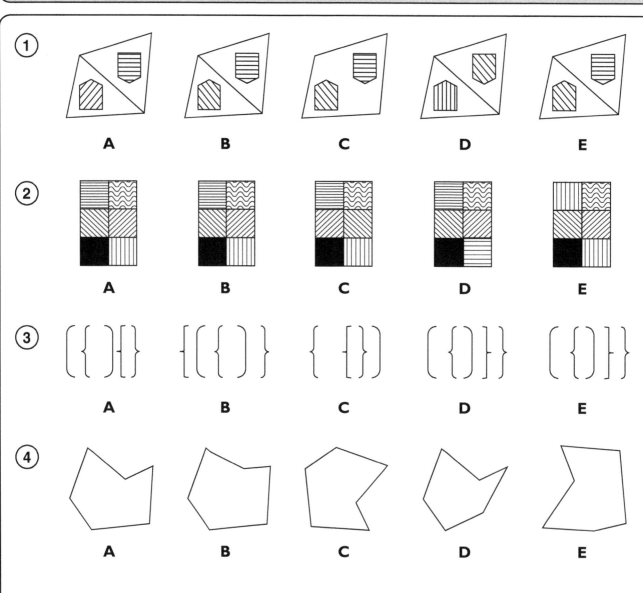

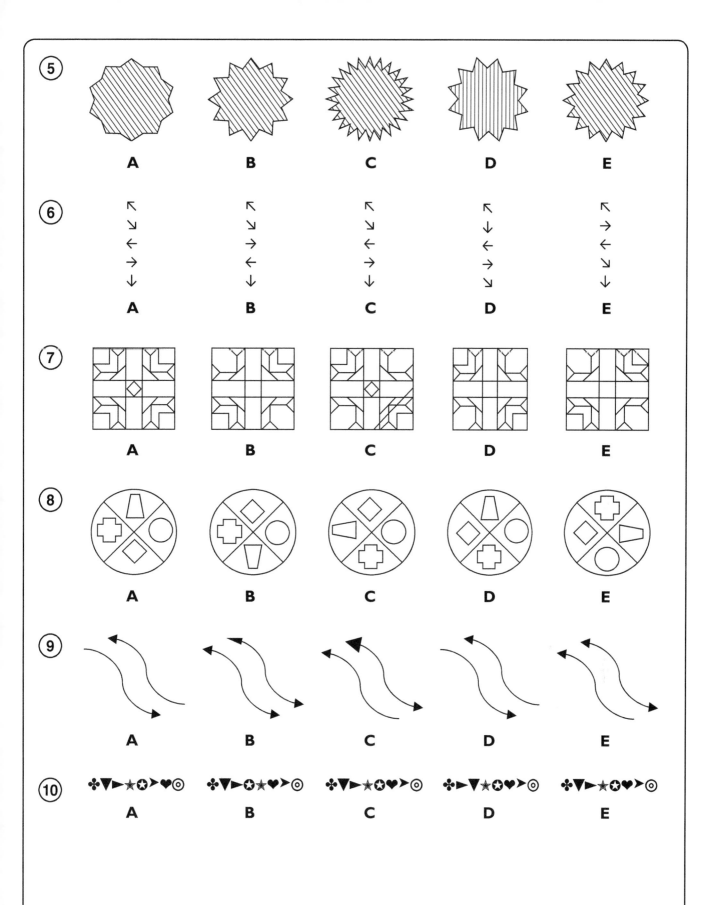

Test 13

You have 5 minutes to complete this test.

You have 10 questions to complete within the given time.

The three figures on the left are similar in some way.

Work out how they are similar and then circle the letter below the figure from the answer choices that goes with them.

EXAMPLE

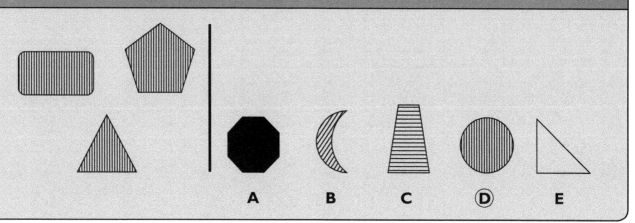

①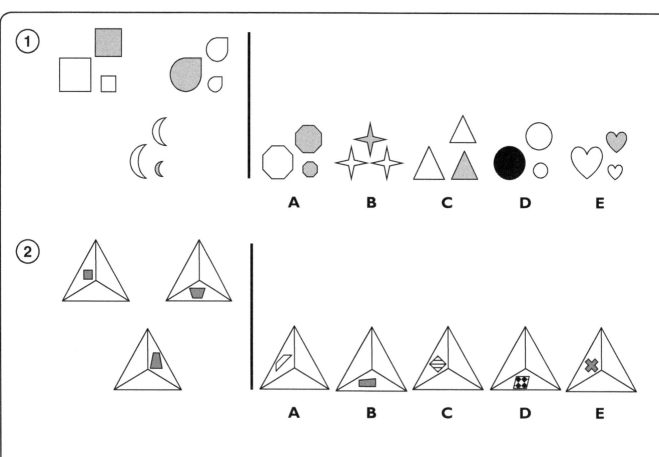

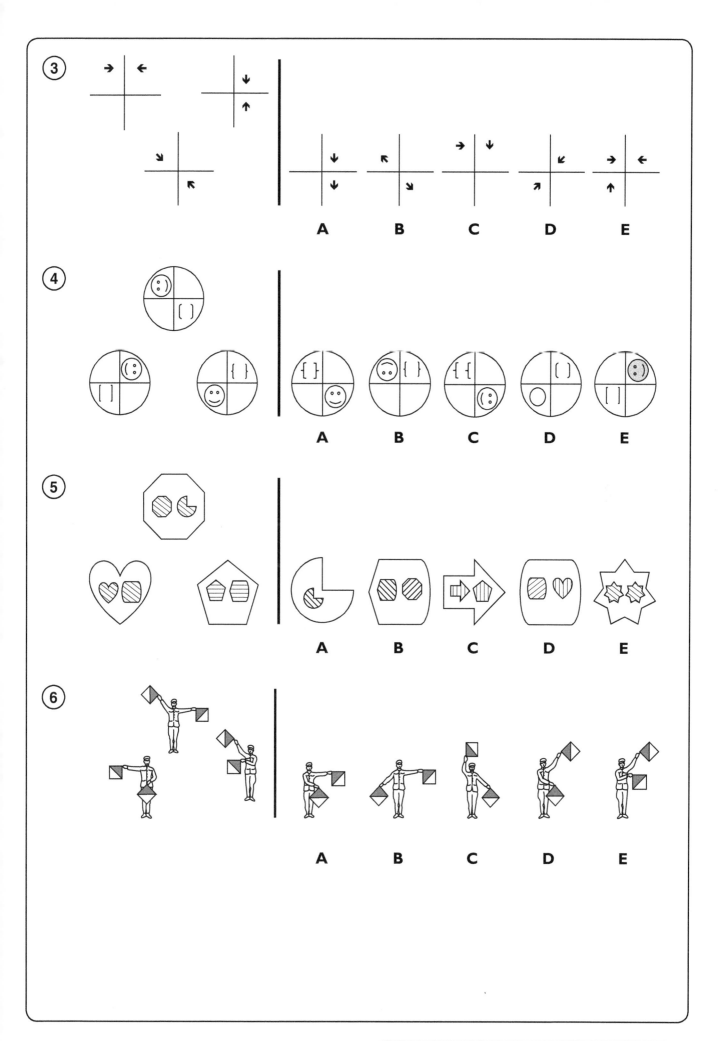

Questions continue on next page

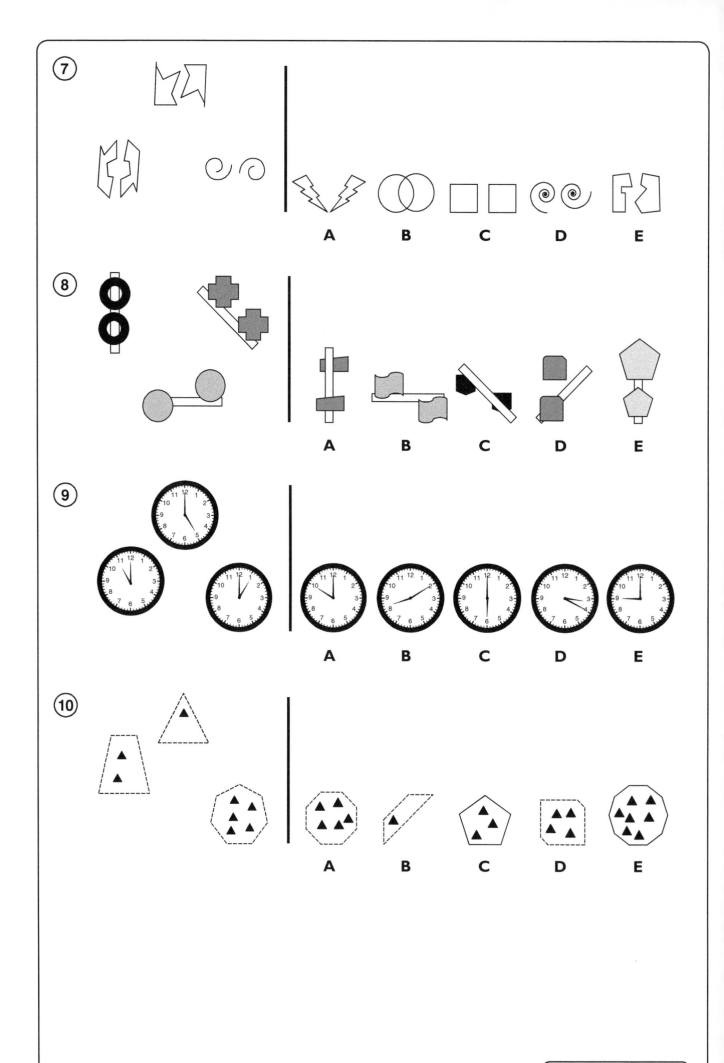

Score: .... / 10

Test 14

Circle the letter below the cube that can be formed by folding the 'net' on the left.

EXAMPLE

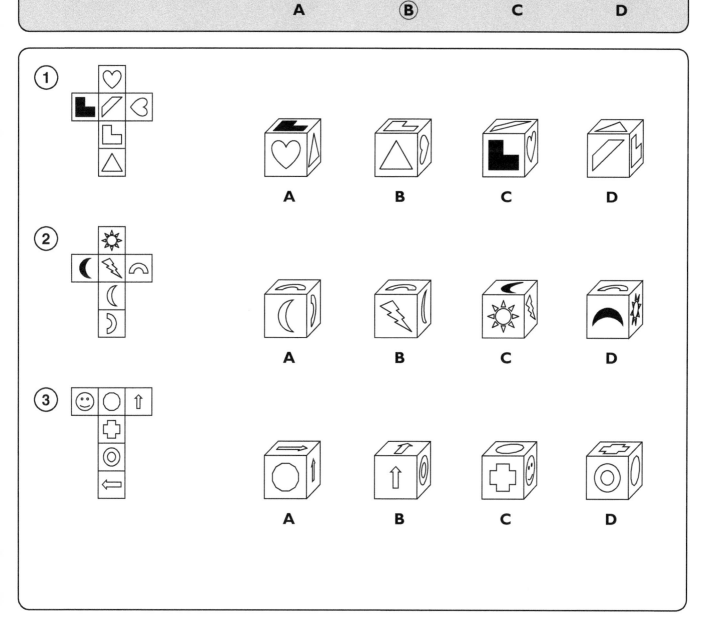

Questions continue on next page

37

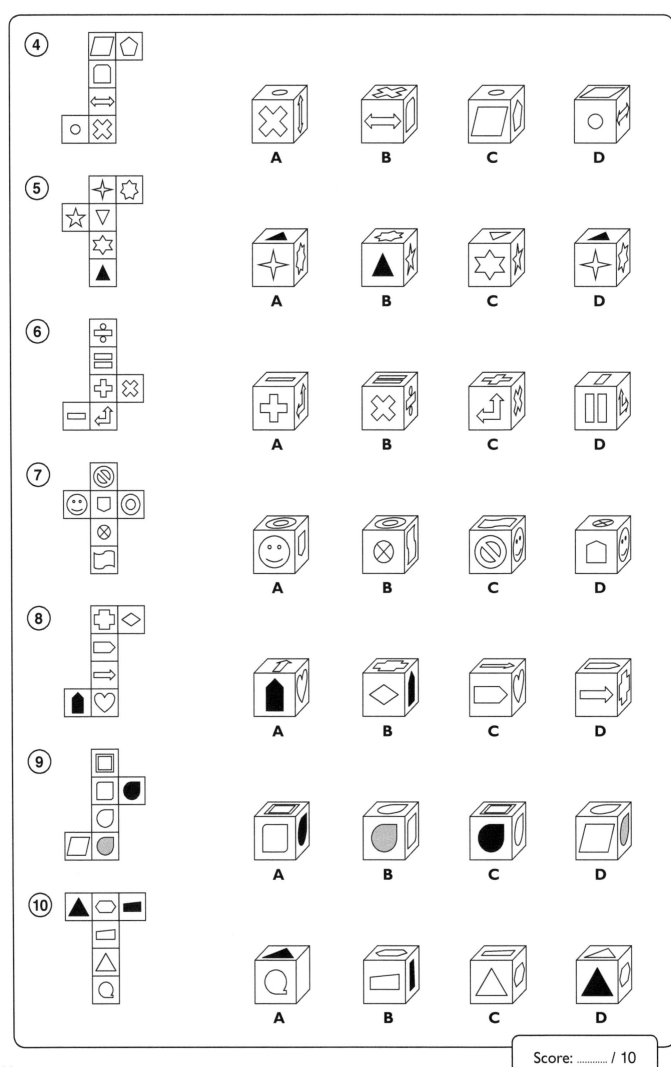

Score: .... / 10

Test 15

You have 5 minutes to complete this test.

You have 10 questions to complete within the given time.

Circle the letter below the figure on the right that shows the top-down, plan view of the 3D figure on the left.

EXAMPLE

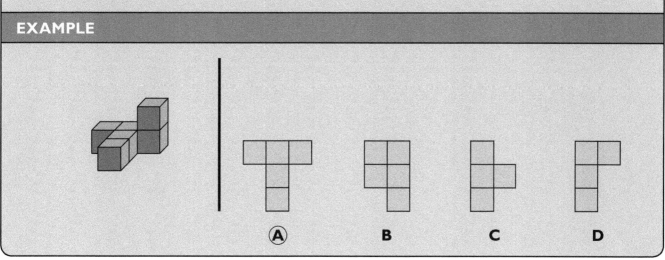

A   B   C   D

①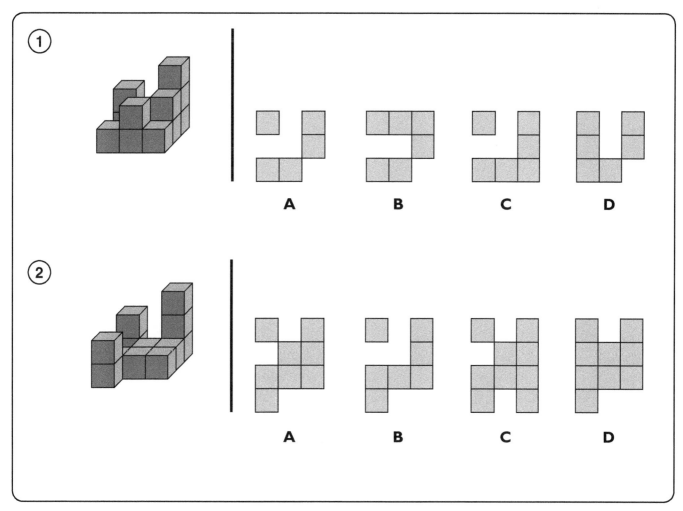

A   B   C   D

②

A   B   C   D

Questions continue on next page

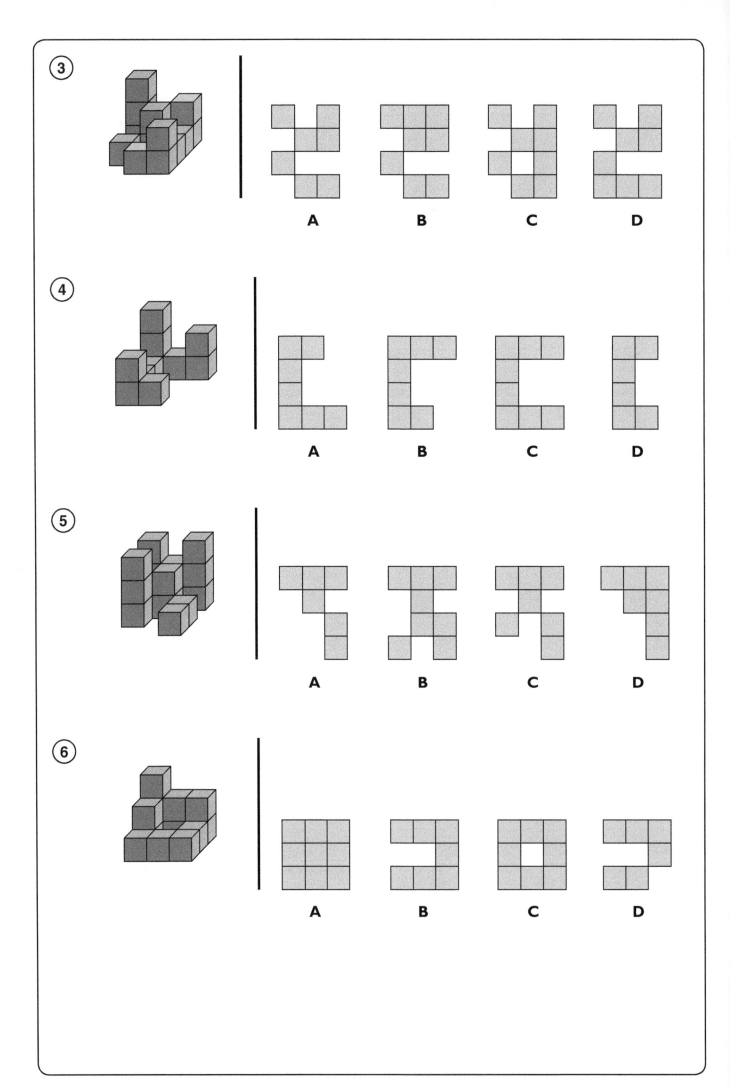

③

A B C D

④

A B C D

⑤

A B C D

⑥

A B C D

40

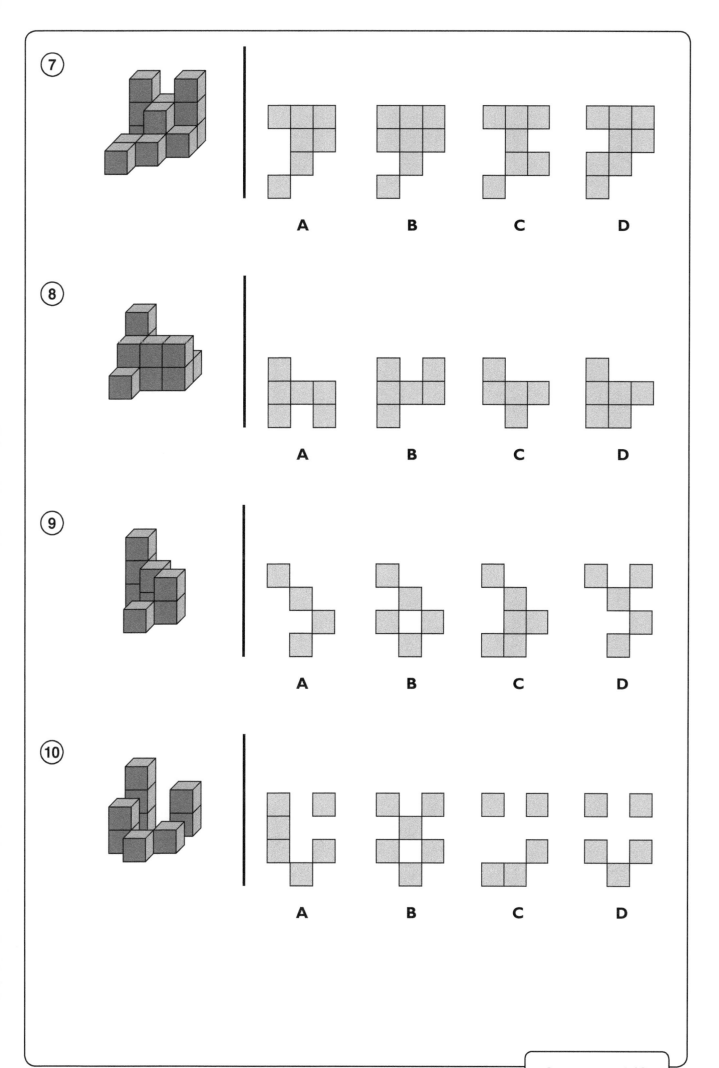

⑦   **A**   **B**   **C**   **D**

⑧   **A**   **B**   **C**   **D**

⑨   **A**   **B**   **C**   **D**

⑩   **A**   **B**   **C**   **D**

Score: .... / 10

41

Test 16

You have 5 minutes to complete this test.

You have 10 questions to complete within the given time.

Circle the letter below the figure on the right that looks like the figure on the left when it is reflected over the line.

A   B   ©   D

①   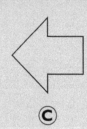

A   B   C   D

②

A   B   C   D

③   

A   B   C   D

④   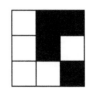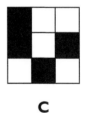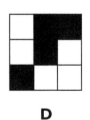

A   B   C   D

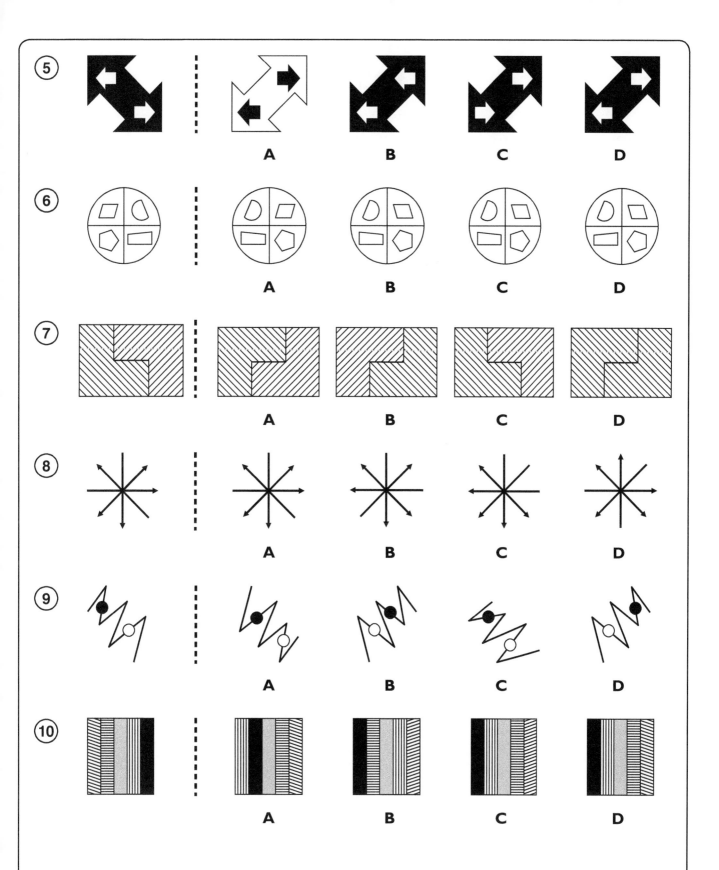

Test 17

You have 5 minutes to complete this test.

You have 10 questions to complete within the given time.

In each question there is a sequence of patterned squares with one missing.

Circle the letter below the square that shows the missing pattern.

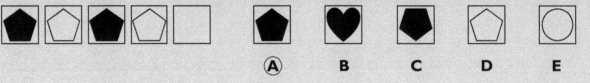

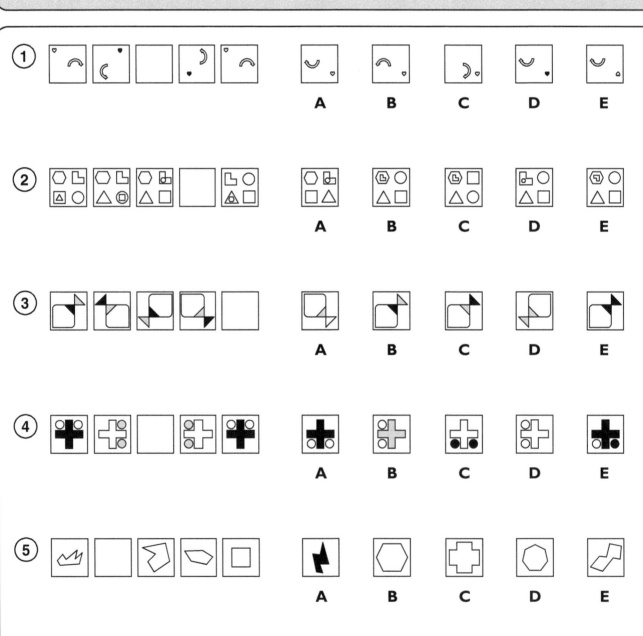

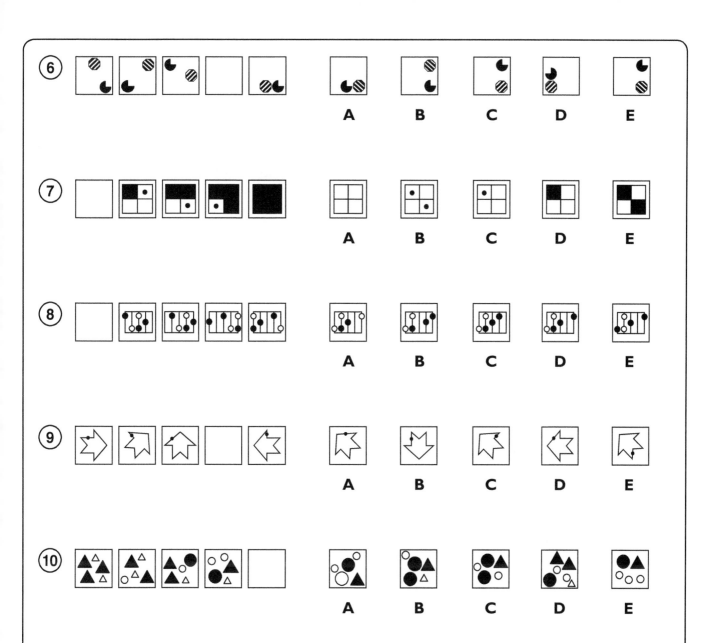

Test 18

You have 5 minutes to complete this test.

You have 10 questions to complete within the given time.

Each figure on the left has a code next to it. The code consists of letters. The figure on the right has no code next to it.

Circle the letter below the code on the right that best describes the figure on the right.

		AZ	BZ	AX	CZ	BY
		A	**B**	**C**	**D**	**(E)**

AZ

AY

BZ

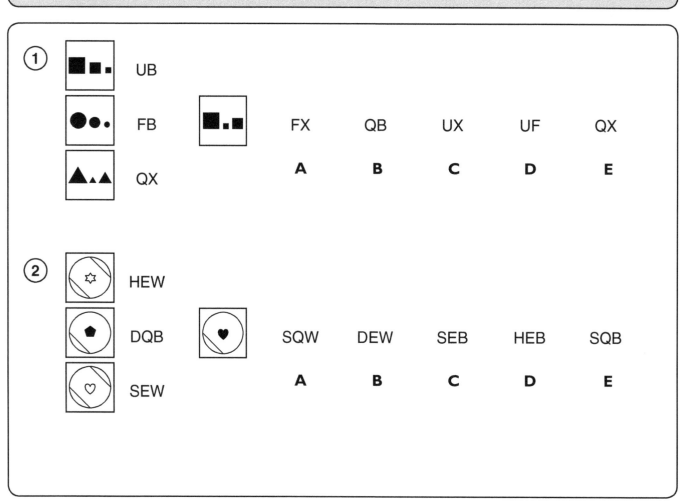

① UB
FB
QX

	FX	QB	UX	UF	QX
	A	**B**	**C**	**D**	**E**

② HEW
DQB
SEW

	SQW	DEW	SEB	HEB	SQB
	A	**B**	**C**	**D**	**E**

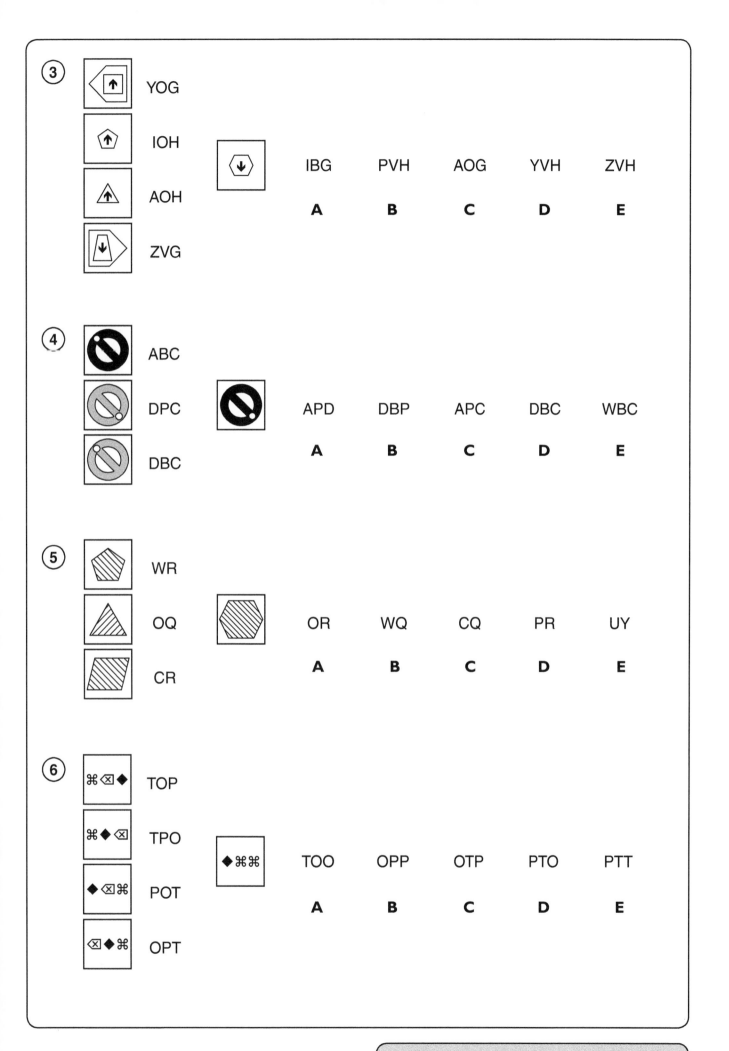

3

| | YOG |
| IOH |
| AOH |
| ZVG |

| | IBG | PVH | AOG | YVH | ZVH |
| | **A** | **B** | **C** | **D** | **E** |

4

| | ABC |
| DPC |
| DBC |

| | APD | DBP | APC | DBC | WBC |
| | **A** | **B** | **C** | **D** | **E** |

5

| | WR |
| OQ |
| CR |

| | OR | WQ | CQ | PR | UY |
| | **A** | **B** | **C** | **D** | **E** |

6

| | TOP |
| TPO |
| POT |
| OPT |

| | TOO | OPP | OTP | PTO | PTT |
| | **A** | **B** | **C** | **D** | **E** |

Questions continue on next page

47

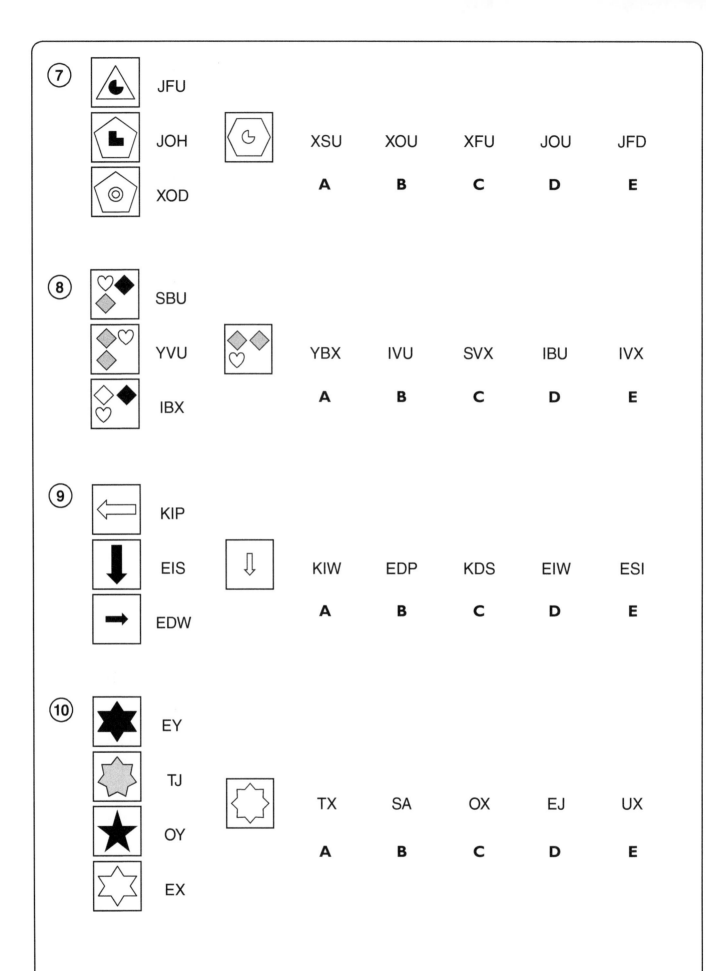

7

JFU			
JOH			
XOD			

XSU   XOU   XFU   JOU   JFD

A   **B**   **C**   **D**   **E**

8

SBU

YVU

IBX

YBX   IVU   SVX   IBU   IVX

A   **B**   **C**   **D**   **E**

9

KIP

EIS

EDW

KIW   EDP   KDS   EIW   ESI

A   **B**   **C**   **D**   **E**

10

EY

TJ

OY

EX

TX   SA   OX   EJ   UX

A   **B**   **C**   **D**   **E**

Score: .... / 10

48

Test 19

There are two figures on the left with an arrow between them. Decide how the second is related to the first.

There is a third figure followed by an arrow and four more figures.

Circle the letter below the figure that is related to the third figure in the same way that the first two figures are related to each other.

EXAMPLE

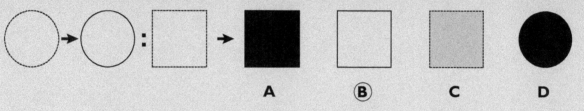

A   (B)   C   D

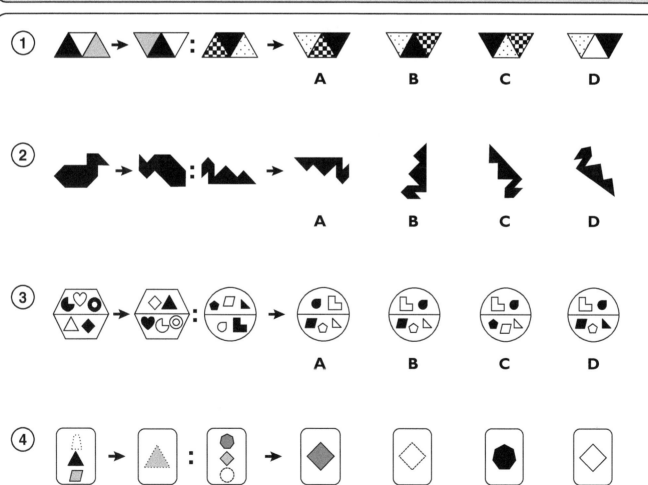

Questions continue on next page

(5)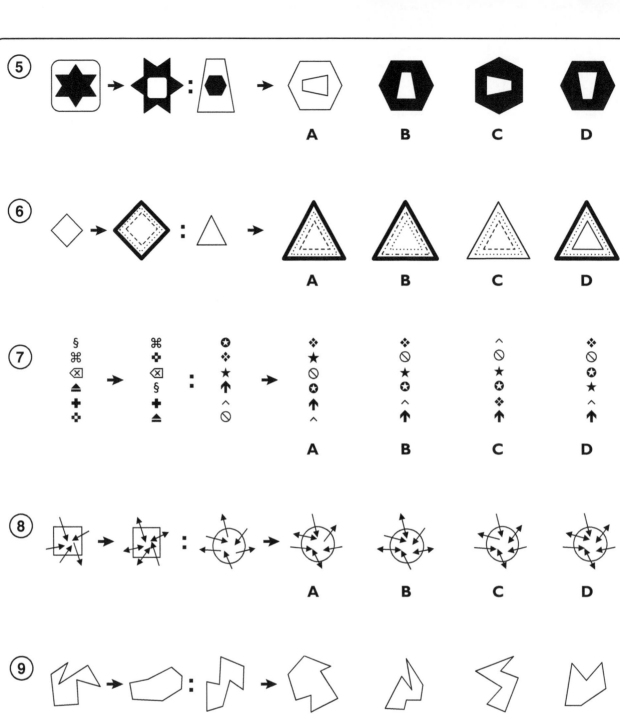

(6)

(7)

(8)

(9)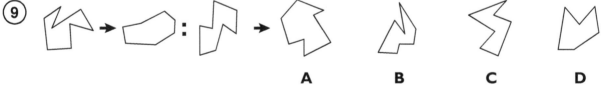

(10)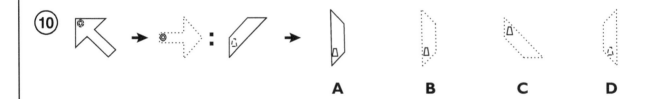

Score: .... / 10

Test 20

You have 5 minutes to complete this test.

You have 10 questions to complete within the given time.

Circle the letter below the figure that is most unlike the others.

EXAMPLE

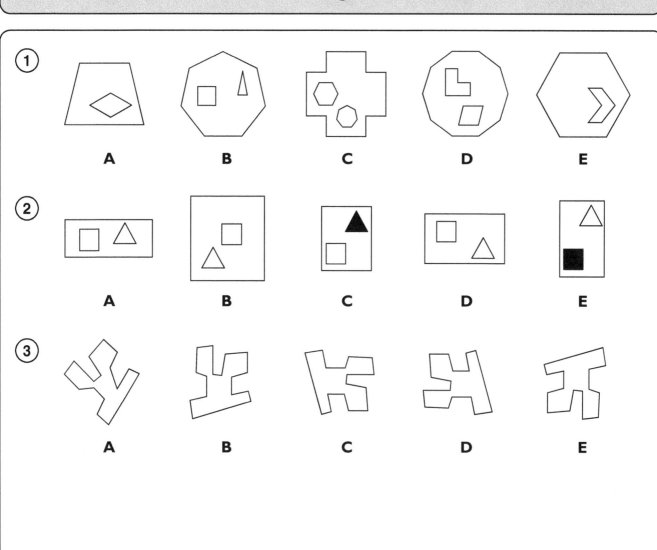

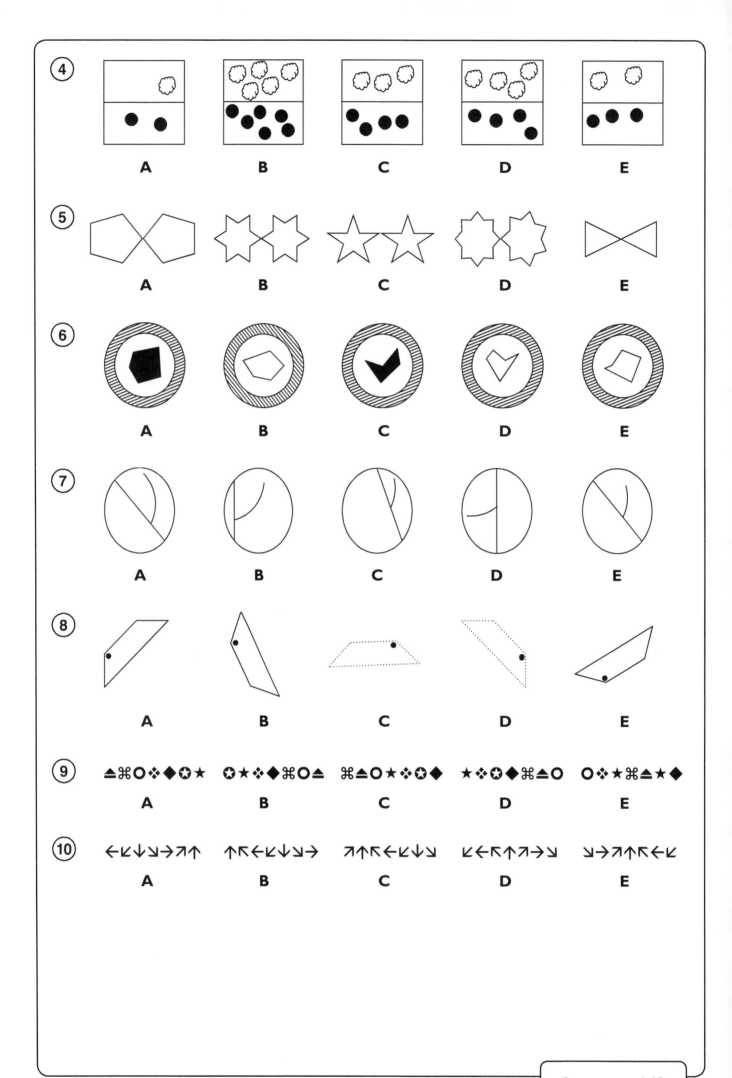

Test 21

You have 5 minutes to complete this test.

You have 10 questions to complete within the given time.

In each question, there are figures arranged in a large square.

One figure is missing and its place is shown by a question mark.

Circle the letter below the answer choice that should replace the question mark.

EXAMPLE

 ?

A   B   Ⓒ   D   E

---

①

 ?

5	4
4	3

4	3
4	3

5	5
3	3

3	5
4	4

5	3
5	5

   A   B   C   D   E

②

 ?

   A   B   C   D   E

Questions continue on next page

53

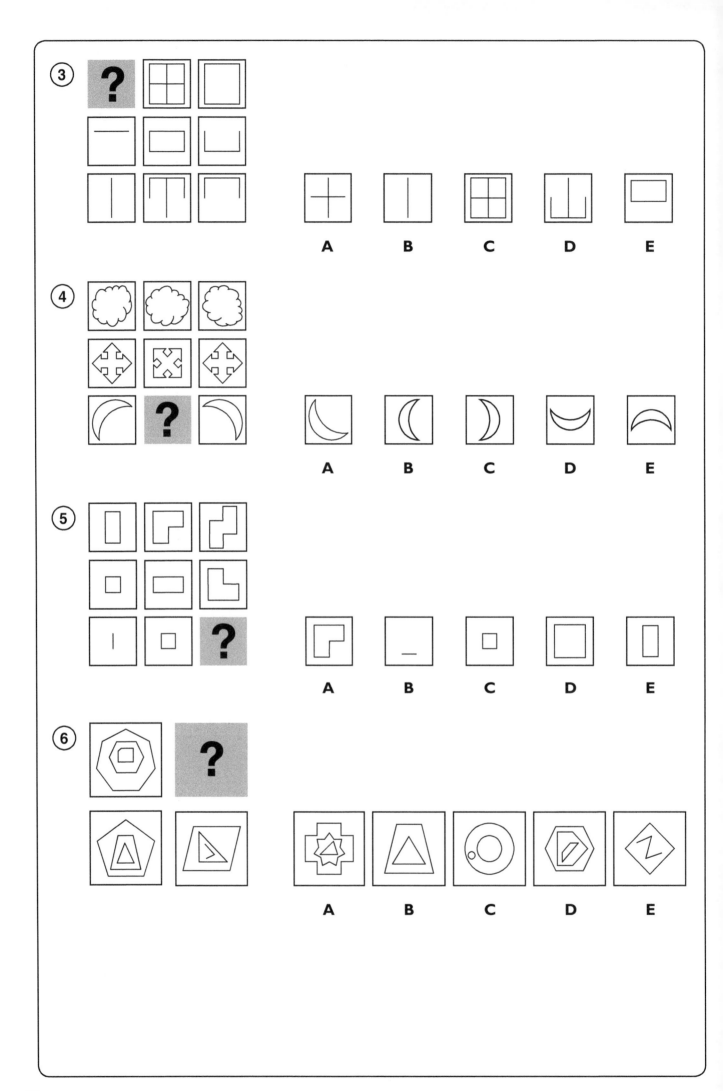

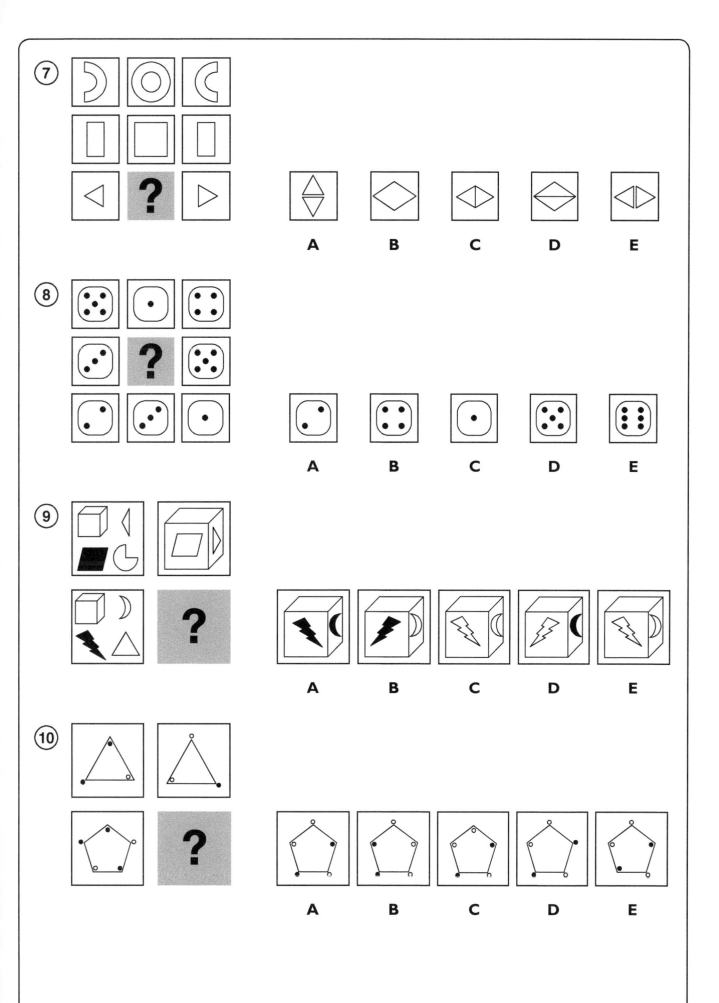

Test 22

You have 5 minutes to complete this test.

You have 10 questions to complete within the given time.

The three figures on the left are similar in some way.

Work out how they are similar and then circle the letter below the figure from the answer choices that goes with them.

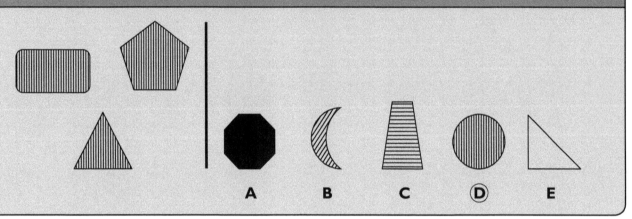

①
$$\frac{6}{3}$$

$$\frac{8}{4} \qquad \frac{2}{1}$$

$\frac{10}{10}$	$\frac{4}{2}$	$\frac{4}{10}$	$\frac{8}{5}$	$\frac{3}{6}$
A	B	C	D	E

②

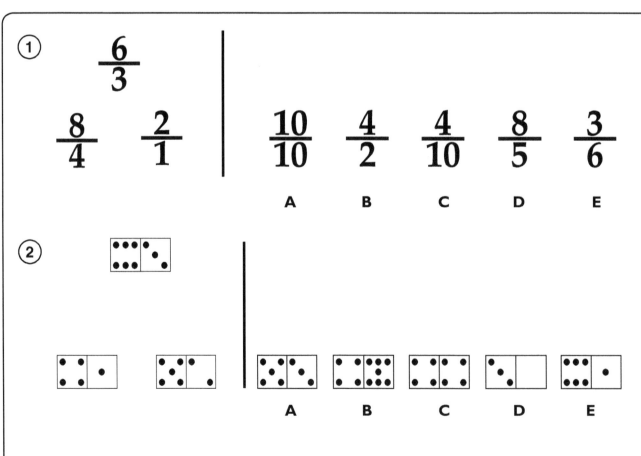

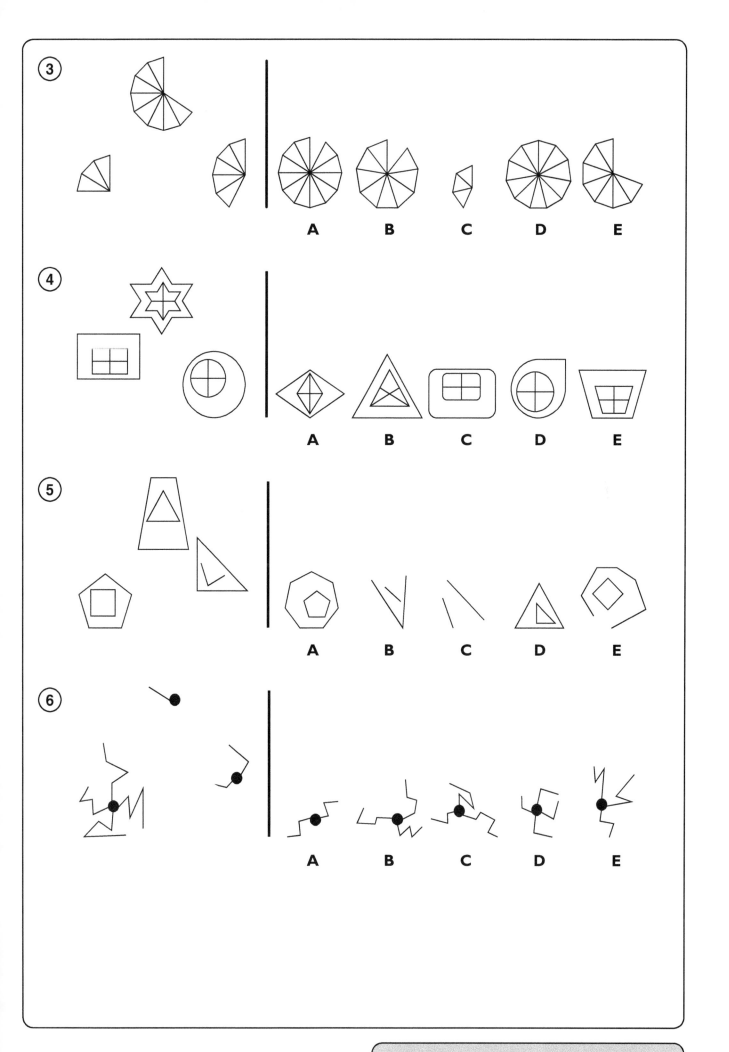

Questions continue on next page

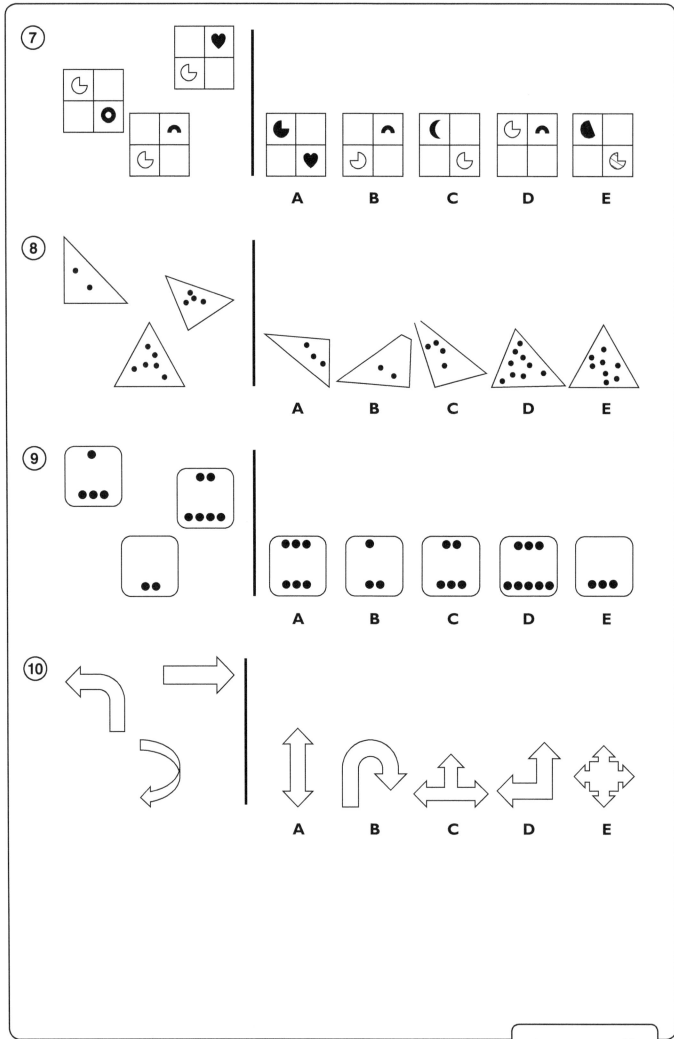

⑦

A B C D E

⑧

A B C D E

⑨

A B C D E

⑩

A B C D E

Score: .... / 10

Test 23

You have 5 minutes to complete this test.

You have 10 questions to complete within the given time.

Circle the letter below the cube that can be formed by folding the 'net' on the left.

A   Ⓑ   C   D

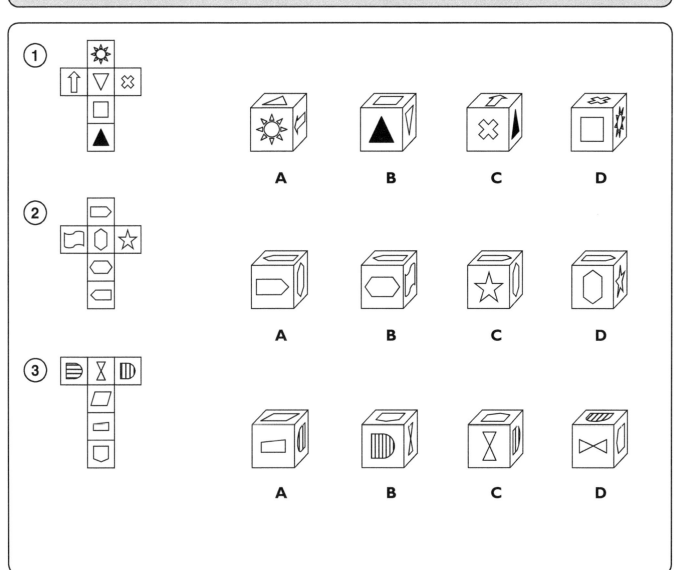

1.
A   B   C   D

2.
A   B   C   D

3.
A   B   C   D

Questions continue on next page

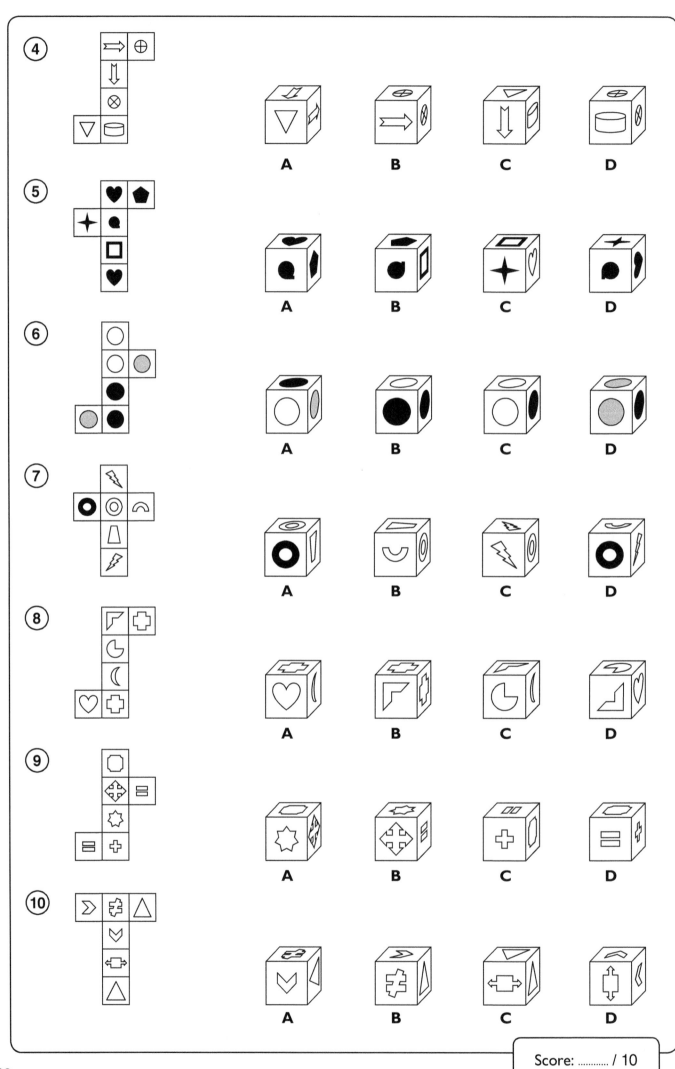

Score: .... / 10

Test 24

Circle the letter below the figure on the right that shows the top-down, plan view of the 3D figure on the left.

EXAMPLE

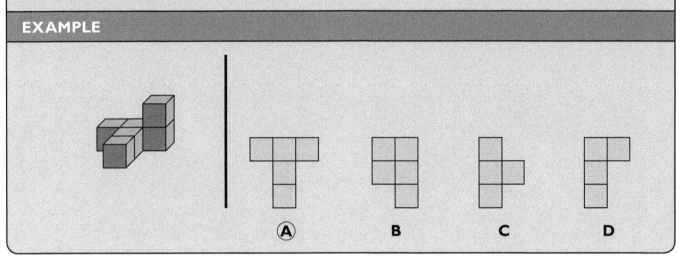

A B C D

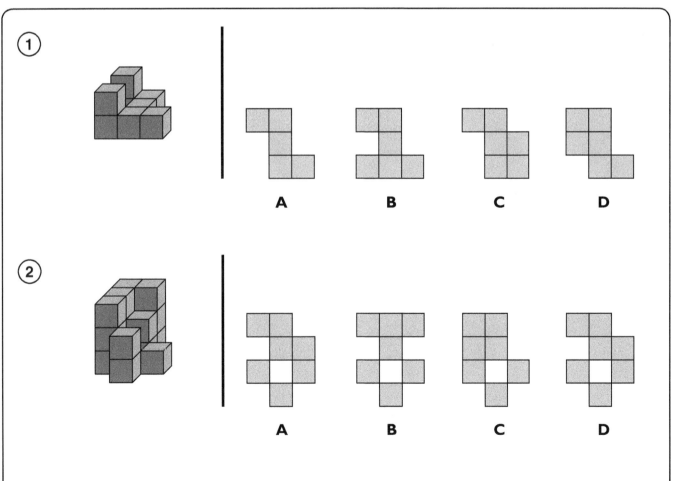

Questions continue on next page

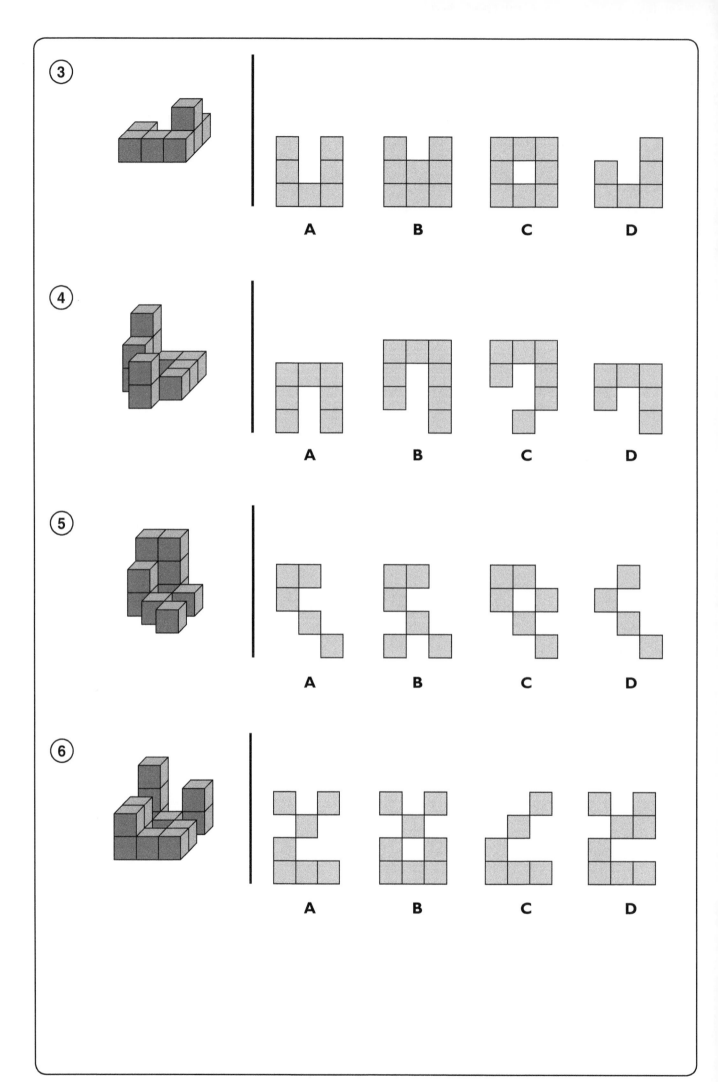

③

A B C D

④

A B C D

⑤

A B C D

⑥

A B C D

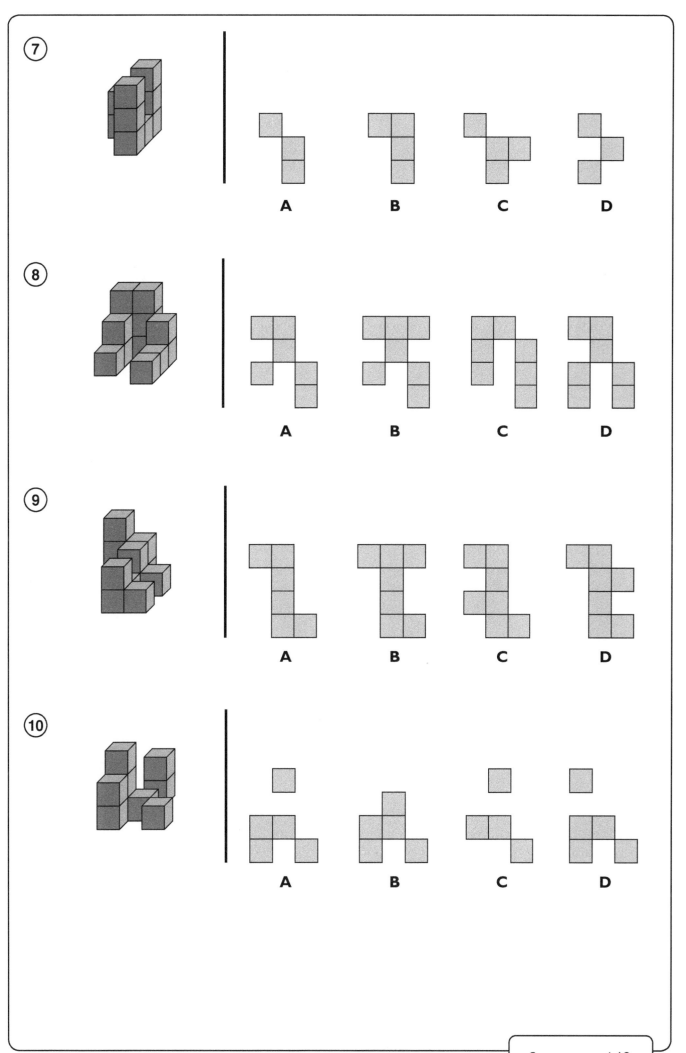

⑦

A B C D

⑧

A B C D

⑨

A B C D

⑩

A B C D

Test 25

You have 5 minutes to complete this test.

You have 10 questions to complete within the given time.

Circle the letter below the figure on the right that looks like the figure on the left when it is reflected over the line.

EXAMPLE

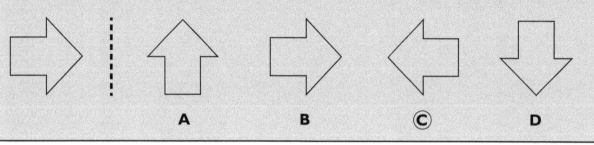

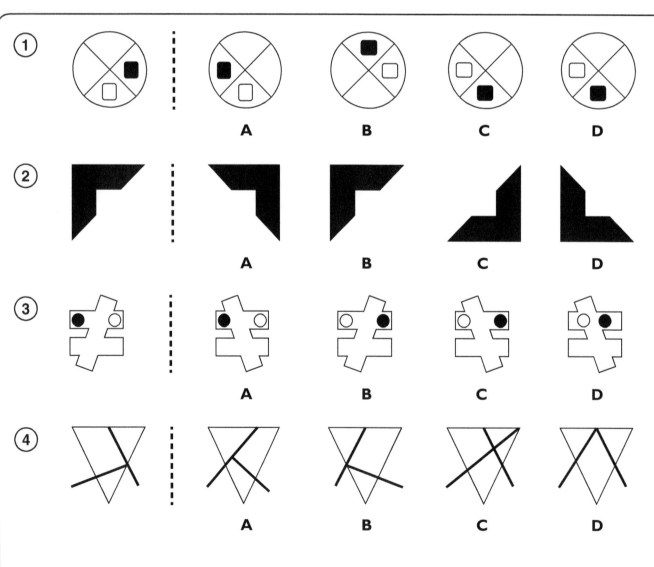

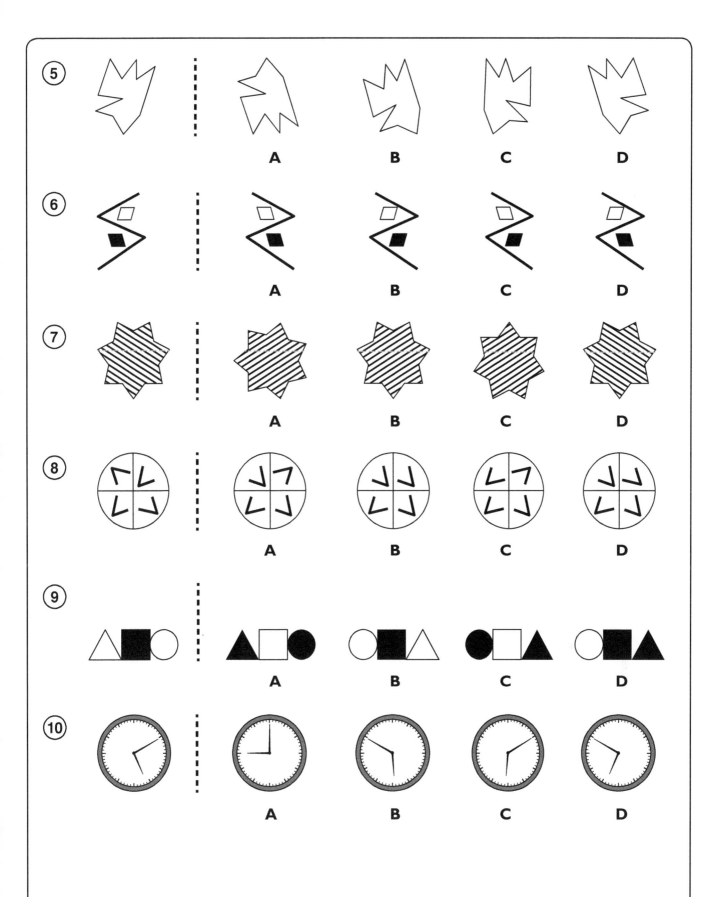

Notes

Answers

Test 1

Q1 E The figure in the top right consists of two identical versions of the arrow in the figure in the top left.

Therefore, the figure in the bottom right should consist of two identical versions of the arrow in the figure in the bottom left.

Therefore, the answer is E.

Q2 D The figure in the top right is a smaller version of the figure in the top left.

Therefore the figure in the bottom right should be a smaller version of the figure in the bottom left.

Therefore, the answer is D.

Q3 F The shading of each quarter moves one place across in a clockwise direction to form the figure in the top right.

Therefore, the shading of each quarter of the circle in the figure in the bottom left should move one place across in a clockwise direction to form the figure in the bottom right.

Therefore, the answer is F.

Q4 B The figure in the top right consists of two reflected versions of the figure in the top left, placed on top of each other.

Therefore, the figure in the bottom right should consist of two reflected versions of the figure in the bottom left, placed on top of each other.

Therefore, the answer is B.

Q5 C The figure in the top left consists of six crosses with black, white or striped shading. The figure in the top right consists of the same crosses but with opposite shading: black crosses become white, white crosses become black and the direction of the stripes switches.

Therefore, the same inverse shading must be applied to the figure in the bottom left to create the figure in the bottom right.

Therefore, the answer is C.

Q6 C The figure in the top right shows the original plus the horizontal reflection of the shaded parts in the figure in the top left.

Therefore, the figure in the bottom right should show the original plus the horizontal reflection of the shaded parts in the figure in the bottom left.

Therefore, the answer is C.

Q7 A Each smaller rectangle in the figure in the top left moves one place to the right to form the figure in the top right.

Therefore, each smaller rectangle in the figure in the bottom right should be moved one place to the left to form the figure in the bottom left.

Therefore, the answer is A.

Q8 F The shape in the figure in the top left is reflected vertically in the figure in the top right.

The arrows in the figure in the top left face the opposite direction in the figure in the top right.

Therefore, these changes must be applied to the figure in the bottom left to form the figure in the bottom right.

Therefore, the answer is F.

Q9 C The positions of the second and third shapes in the figure in the top left are switched in the figure in the top right.

The gaps between the shapes in the figure in the top left are removed in the figure in the top right.

These changes must be applied to the figure in the bottom left to form the figure in the bottom right.

Therefore, the answer is C.

Q10 A The shapes in the figure in the top left are rearranged in the figure in the top right.

Therefore, the shapes in the figure in the bottom left should be rearranged in the same way to form the figure in the bottom right.

Therefore, the answer is A.

Test 2

Q1 **C** and **E**

Q2 **A** and **B**

Q3 **C** and **E**

Q4 **D** and **E**

Q5 **B** and **C**

Q6 **A** and **D**

Q7 **A** and **E**

Q8 **B** and **C**

Q9 **A** and **C**

Q10 **B** and **D**

Test 3

Q1 **B** The figures on the left are each rotations of the same shape.

Therefore, the answer is B.

Q2 **A** The figures on the left each have six sides.

Therefore, the answer is A.

Q3 **E** The figures on the left are each rotations of the same shape.

Therefore, the answer is E.

Q4 **D** The figures on the left each consist of a large shape with a small square above it. The large shape and the square have opposite black and white shading.

Therefore, the answer is D.

Q5 **C** The figures on the left each consist of a larger white shape containing a smaller black version of the same shape.

The black version of the shape is a reflection of the larger white shape in a vertical mirror line.

Therefore, the answer is C.

Q6 **C** The figures on the left each consist of three shapes. In each figure, the black shape lies on top of the white shape and the white shape lies on top of the grey shape.

Therefore, the answer is C.

Q7 **B** The figures on the left each consist of a white shape and a 90° clockwise rotation of this white shape next to each other.

Therefore, the answer is B.

Q8 **E** The figures on the left each contain the same three symbols. Each figure contains 12 symbols in total, divided into rows of 3, 4 and 5 symbols.

Therefore, the answer is E.

Q9 **D** The figures on the left each contain two shapes. The smaller internal shape has one side less than the larger external shape. The direction of the line shading in the smaller shape is the same in each figure.

Therefore, the answer is D.

Q10 **A** The figures on the left each contain two circles. In total, any four out of eight quarters in these two circles are shaded black.

Therefore, the answer is A.

Test 4

Q1 **B**

Q2 **A**

Q3 **C**

Q4 **E**

Q5 **C**

Q6 **A**

Q7 **C**

Q8 **B**

Q9 **A**

Q10 **B**

Test 5

Q1 **C**

Q2 **B**

Q3 **C**

Q4 **A**

Q5 **A**

Q6 **D**

Q7 **C**

Q8 **B**

Q9 **D**

Q10 **A**

Test 6

Q1 D

Q2 C

Q3 C

Q4 C

Q5 A

Q6 D

Q7 B

Q8 A

Q9 B

Q10 D

Test 7

Q1 F From left to right, the black outer figure rotates 45° in a clockwise direction whilst the straight line rotates 45° in an anticlockwise direction.

Therefore, the answer is F.

Q2 D From the first box to the second, the outer shape changes from black to white and the inner shape changes from white to black and reflects in a horizontal mirror line. Therefore, the same changes must occur between the third and fourth boxes.

Therefore, the answer is D.

Q3 A Each box contains one black square that is then removed from the next box.

Therefore, the answer is A.

Q4 C Each box contains a figure made from three overlapping versions of the same shape. From left to right, the figures rotate 45° in a clockwise direction and alternate between consisting of two white shapes and one black shape and two black shapes and one white shape. The white shapes always lie on top of the black shapes.

Therefore, the answer is C.

Q5 B From left to right, the rhombus alternates between two positions and the shapes inside the rhombus rotate 90° in an anticlockwise direction with alternate black and white shading.

Therefore, the answer is B.

Q6 E From left to right, the shapes in each box are reflected in alternating vertical and horizontal mirror lines. The pentagon also alternates between black and white shading.

Therefore, the answer is E.

Q7 A From left to right, a black block is added to the figure on the left of each box. The block that was black in the preceding box contains a black circle. The figure on the right of each box alternates between two positions.

Therefore, the answer is A.

Q8 F From left to right, the time moves forward 1 hour and 25 minutes.

Therefore, the answer is F.

Q9 B From left to right, the sum of the dots on the two dice decreases by two.

Therefore, the answer is B.

Q10 E From left to right, the white shape moves in half-length units in a clockwise direction and the circle moves in full-length units in an anticlockwise direction.

Therefore, the answer is E.

Test 8

Q1 C The first letter signifies the shading of the triangle on the left and the second letter signifies the form of the shape on the right.

T = the triangle on the left is shaded black

U = the triangle on the left is shaded white

R = the shape on the right is ⌒

I = the shape on the right is a heart

W = the shape on the right is a trapezium

Therefore, the code of the figure on the right must be TS as the triangle on the left is shaded black and the shape on the right does not match any of the ones in the figures on the left so it must be represented by a new letter.

Test 8 answers continue on next page

Q2 **E** The first letter signifies the form of the outer shape, the second letter signifies the form of the inner shape and the third letter signifies the shading of the outer shape.

Z = outer shape is a square

P = outer shape is a circle

W = outer shape is ◖

A = inner shape is a white heart

B = inner shape is a white triangle

O = outer shape is shaded black

T = outer shape is shaded white

Therefore, the code for the figure on the right is PBT.

Q3 **C** The first letter signifies the type of line and the second letter signifies the form of the shape.

C = dotted line

S = solid line

Y = dashed line

D = square

W = rotated square

P = trapezium

Therefore, the code for the figure on the right is YD.

Q4 **E** The first letter signifies whether the first die is odd or even and the second letter signifies whether the second die is odd or even.

A = first die is even

B = first die is odd

C = second die is even

D = second die is odd

Therefore, the code for the figure on the right is BC.

Q5 **A** The first letter signifies the position of the rectangle and the second letter signifies if the rectangle is shaded.

T = rectangle is on the top

L = rectangle is on the left

R = rectangle is on the right

C = rectangle is shaded

V = rectangle is not shaded

Therefore, the code for the figure on the right is BV as the rectangle is on the bottom so the first letter cannot be T, L or R and the rectangle is not shaded so the second letter must be V.

Q6 **D** The first letter signifies how many parts are shaded and the second letter signifies how many parts the circle is divided into.

R = 2 parts shaded

D = 3 parts shaded

A = 1 part shaded

U = circle divided into 5 parts

P = circle divided into 4 parts

W = circle divided into 3 parts

Therefore, the code for the figure on the right is AP.

Q7 **D** The first letter signifies the shading of the bottom row and the second letter signifies the shading of the top row.

F = bottom row is black, black, white

U = bottom row is black, white, black

I = bottom row is white, black, white

Z = top row is all white

Q = top row is all black

Therefore, the code for the figure on the right is FQ.

Q8 **A** The first letter signifies whether there is a black circle, the second letter signifies the type of line and the third letter signifies the position of the cube.

D = contains black circle

E = no black circles

R = dashed lines

W = solid lines

Q = cube angled to the left

C = cube angled to the right

Therefore, the code for the figure on the right is ERC.

Q9 **C** The first letter signifies the position of the small arrow and the second letter signifies the shading of the large arrow.

D = small arrow in the top right

A = no small arrow

Y = small arrow in the bottom right

W = large arrow has striped shading

Q = large arrow is shaded black

Z = large arrow is shaded white

Therefore, the code for the figure on the right is AZ.

Q10 B The first letter signifies the border type of the shape, the second letter signifies the shading of the shape and the third letter signifies how many sides the shape has.

Y = dashed line border

H = solid line border

G = grey shading

K = white shading

T = shape has three sides

S = shape has four sides

Therefore, the code for the figure on the right is HKS.

Test 9

Q1 C The figure is reflected in a vertical mirror line.

Q2 A The large grey shape changes into two smaller overlapping versions of itself. The black version lies on top of the white version.

Q3 A The five shapes in the pentagon in the first figure are rearranged in the second figure. The five shapes in the pentagon in the third figure must be rearranged in the same way to find the answer.

Q4 C The number of black circles and the number of sides of the shape switch with each other.

Q5 D The time moves forward by 20 minutes.

Q6 C The sum of the dots shown on the die decreases by one.

Q7 B The striped shading of the larger shape changes direction. The smaller shape changes from black to white and rotates 180°.

Q8 C The number of squares decreases by one.

Q9 D The number of points on the star decreases by two.

Q10 A The top shape is in the middle, the middle shape is on the right and the bottom shape is on the left.

The shading of the top shape matches the shading of the shape on the left.

The shading of the middle shape matches the shading of the shape in the middle.

The shading of the bottom shape matches the shading of the shape on the right.

Test 10

Q1 E In all other figures, the internal rectangle is the same size.

Q2 E In all other figures, the internal shape is a smaller vertical reflection of the larger external shape.

Q3 C All the figures consist of one large shape and two smaller versions of the same shape. However, in all the figures except C, the smaller black shape lies on top of the larger shape and the smaller white shape lies below the larger shape.

Q4 E All other figures consist of exactly three straight lines.

Q5 E In all other figures, there are two arrows facing in the opposite direction to each other.

Q6 E In all other figures, the arrow divides the shape into two equal parts.

Q7 D In all other figures, the × and the @ are in the same horizontal row.

Q8 C In all other figures, the number of small black squares equals the number of lines passing through the large shape.

Q9 A All the other figures are rotations of the same shape.

Q10 A All figures consist of a white shape placed upon a black shape. In all figures except figure A, the white shape and the black shape are the same size.

Test 11

Q1 A The figure in the top right rearranges the order and number of the symbols in the figure in the top left.

Therefore, the order and number of the symbols in the figure in the bottom left should be rearranged in the same way to form the figure in the bottom right.

Therefore, the answer is A.

Test 11 answers continue on next page

Q2　B　From left to right, the open figures in each row consist of one line less than the preceding figure.

This pattern must be applied to the middle row to find the open figure in the centre.

Therefore, the answer is B.

Q3　C　The figure in the top right consists of the same shapes as the figure in the top left. However, the diagonally opposite shapes have switched places and the shading on the two striped shapes has also switched.

Therefore, these changes must be applied to the figure in the bottom left to form the figure in the bottom right.

Therefore, the answer is C.

Q4　D　The figure in the bottom right rearranges the order and size of the shapes in the figure in the bottom left.

Therefore, the same rearrangement must be applied to the figure in the top left to form the figure in the top right.

Therefore, the answer is D.

Q5　B　Each row consists of three versions of the same shape and a total of six halves. In each row, two of the six halves are shaded grey.

Since one half is already shaded in the bottom row, the figure in the bottom left should have one half shaded grey.

Therefore, the answer is B.

Q6　A　The figure in the top right consists of the same shapes in the figure in the top left but with opposite shading and size. The large shapes have become small and the small shapes have become large. The black shapes have become white and the white shapes have become black.

Therefore, the same changes must be applied to the figure in the bottom left to form the figure in the bottom right.

Therefore, the answer is A.

Q7　B　In each column, the number of black circles can be subtracted from the number of grey circles to give the number of white circles.

Therefore, the missing figure must consist of 1 white circle as 4 (grey) − 3 (black) = 1 (white).

Therefore, the answer is B.

Q8　D　The figure in the top right is a narrower version of the figure in the top left.

Therefore, the figure in the bottom right must be a narrower version of the figure in the bottom left.

Therefore, the answer is D.

Q9　B　The third figure in each row shows the combination of the first two figures in the row.

Therefore, the figure in the top left must be the part missing from the combination in the figure in the top right.

Therefore, the answer is B.

Q10　F　The figure in the top right is formed by rotating the figure in the top left 90° clockwise.

Therefore, the figure in the bottom right is formed by rotating the figure in the bottom left in the same way.

Therefore, the answer is F.

Test 12

Q1　B and E

Q2　A and B

Q3　D and E

Q4　A and C

Q5　B and D

Q6　A and C

Q7　B and D

Q8　A and E

Q9　A and D

Q10　C and E

Test 13

Q1　E　The figures on the left each consist of three different-sized versions of the same shape. Two of the versions are white and one is grey.

Therefore, the answer is E.

Q2　B　The figures on the left each consist of a triangle divided into three parts. One part contains a quadrilateral shaded in grey.

Therefore, the answer is B.

Q3 **D** The figures on the left each consist of a cross and two arrows that are pointing at each other.

Therefore, the answer is D.

Q4 **A** The figures on the left each consist of a circle divided into four equal sections. One section contains a white face and the diagonally opposite section contains two brackets facing each other.

Therefore, the answer is A.

Q5 **C** The figures on the left each consist of a large shape and two smaller shapes. The smaller shape on the left is a smaller version of the large shape. Both of the smaller shapes are shaded with stripes in the same direction.

Therefore, the answer is C.

Q6 **C** The figures on the left each show a man holding a flag in each hand. In each figure, the flag in the man's right hand is held higher than the flag in the man's left hand.

Therefore, the answer is C.

Q7 **C** The figures on the left each consist of two versions of the same shape next to each other but not touching. One of the shapes is rotated 180°.

Therefore, the answer is C.

Q8 **B** The figures on the left each consist of two identical shapes placed upon a white rectangle.

Therefore, the answer is B.

Q9 **E** The figures on the left are each clocks showing the time at an odd-numbered hour.

Therefore, the answer is E.

Q10 **D** The figures on the left each consist of a shape containing a number of black triangles. Each shape has dashed sides and the number of triangles it contains is two less than its number of sides.

Therefore, the answer is D.

Test 14

Q1	**B**
Q2	**D**
Q3	**B**
Q4	**A**

Q5	**A**
Q6	**C**
Q7	**B**
Q8	**A**
Q9	**A**
Q10	**B**

Test 15

Q1	**C**
Q2	**A**
Q3	**C**
Q4	**B**
Q5	**C**
Q6	**C**
Q7	**D**
Q8	**B**
Q9	**A**
Q10	**D**

Test 16

Q1	**C**
Q2	**D**
Q3	**B**
Q4	**A**
Q5	**D**
Q6	**B**
Q7	**A**
Q8	**B**
Q9	**D**
Q10	**C**

Test 17

Q1 **A** From left to right, the heart symbol moves in a clockwise direction from corner to corner and alternates between black and white shading. From left to right, the arrow reflects through a diagonal mirror line.

Therefore, the answer is A.

Test 17 answers continue on next page

Q2 **B** Each box contains four similar-sized shapes and one smaller shape. From left to right, the smaller shape moves in an anticlockwise direction from one shape to another. In subsequent boxes, the smaller shape replaces the shape it is inside and the replaced shape then becomes the smaller shape.

Therefore, the answer is B.

Q3 **B** From left to right, the figure in each box reflects in alternating vertical and horizontal mirror lines. The shading of the two triangles also alternates.

Therefore, the answer is B.

Q4 **A** From left to right, the cross alternates between black and white shading and the circles alternate between grey and white shading. The circles rotate around the cross in a clockwise direction

Therefore, the answer is A.

Q5 **D** From left to right, the number of sides of the shape in each box decreases by one.

Therefore, the answer is D.

Q6 **E** From left to right, the octagon moves in half-length units in a clockwise direction. The direction of its striped shading also alternates. From left to right, the black shape moves in full-length units in a clockwise direction.

Therefore, the answer is E.

Q7 **C** From left to right, the small black circle rotates around the squares in a clockwise direction. The square that contains the circle is shaded black in the next box.

Therefore, the answer is C.

Q8 **D** From left to right, the circles move one column to the right from one box to the next.

Therefore, the answer is D.

Q9 **A** From left to right, the arrow rotates 45° in an anticlockwise direction. The black circle moves along the sides of the arrow in a clockwise direction.

Therefore, the answer is A.

Q10 **C** From left to right in alternating boxes, a large black triangle is replaced by a small white circle and then a small white triangle is replaced by a large black circle.

Therefore, the answer is C.

Test 18

Q1 **C** The first letter signifies the form of the shapes and the second letter signifies the order of the shapes.

U = squares

F = circles

Q = triangles

B = ordered from largest to smallest

X = ordered largest then smallest then middle-sized

Therefore, the code for the figure on the right is UX.

Q2 **E** The first letter signifies the form of the shape in the circle, the second letter signifies the number of lines in the circle and the third letter signifies the shading of the shape in the circle.

H = star

D = pentagon

S = heart

E = two lines in the circle

Q = one line in the circle

W = shape in the circle shaded white

B = shape in the circle shaded black

Therefore, the code for the figure on the right is SQB.

Q3 **B** The first letter signifies the form of the shape around the arrow, the second letter signifies the direction of the arrow and the third letter signifies the presence of a second shape.

Y = square

I = pentagon

A = triangle

Z = trapezium

O = arrow pointing up

V = arrow pointing down

G = two shapes around the arrow

H = one shape around the arrow

Therefore, the code for the figure on the right is PVH. Since the shape around the arrow is a hexagon, the first letter cannot be Y (square) or Z (trapezium), ruling out options **D** and **E**.

Q4 **C** The first letter signifies the shading of the shape, the second letter signifies the position of the white circle and the third letter signifies the form of the shape.

A = shaded black

D = shaded grey

B = white circle in the top half of the shape

P = white circle in the bottom half of the shape

C = shape is ⦾

Therefore, the code for the figure on the right is APC.

Q5 **D** The first letter signifies the form of the shape and the second letter signifies the direction of the line shading.

W = pentagon

O = triangle

C = rhombus

R = line shading from top to bottom

Q = line shading from bottom to top

Therefore, the code for the figure on the right is PR. The figure on the right is a hexagon so the first letter cannot be O (triangle), ruling out option **A**.

Q6 **E** The first letter signifies the first symbol, the second letter signifies the second symbol and the third letter signifies the third symbol.

T = ⌘

P = ♦

O = ⌫

Therefore, the code for the figure on the right is PTT.

Q7 **A** The first letter signifies the shading of the inner shape, the second letter signifies the form of the outer shape and the third letter signifies the form of the inner shape.

J = inner shape shaded black

X = inner shape shaded white

F = outer shape is a triangle

O = outer shape is a pentagon

U = inner shape is ◔

H = inner shape is ⌐

D = inner shape is ◎

Therefore, the code for the figure on the right is XSU. The outer shape is a hexagon so the second letter cannot be O (pentagon) or F (triangle), ruling out options **B** and **C**.

Q8 **B** The first letter signifies the position of the two squares, the second letter signifies the presence of a black shape and the third letter signifies the number of white shapes.

S = one square in bottom left and one square in top right

Y = one square in bottom left and one square in top left

I = one square in top left and one square in top right

B = figure contains a black shape

V = figure does not contain a black shape

U = figure contains one white shape

X = figure contains two white shapes

Therefore, the code for the figure on the right is IVU.

Q9 **C** The first letter signifies the shading of the arrow, the second letter indicates the size of the arrow and the third letter indicates the direction of the arrow.

K = arrow shaded white

E = arrow shaded black

I = large arrow

D = small arrow

P = arrow facing west

S = arrow facing south

W = arrow facing east

Therefore, the code for the figure on the right is KDS.

Test 18 answers continue on next page

Q10 E The first letter signifies the number of points the star has and the second letter signifies the shading of the star.

E = star has 6 points

T = star has 7 points

O = star has 5 points

Y = star is shaded black

J = star is shaded grey

X = star is shaded white

The star on the right has 8 points so the first letter of its code cannot be E, T or O. It is shaded white so the second letter of its code must be X. The correct answer is therefore a code which does not have E, T or O as the first letter and has X as the second letter.

Therefore, the code for the figure on the right is UX.

Test 19

Q1 A The figure is reflected through a horizontal mirror line. The shading of each triangle moves one triangle to the right.

Q2 C The figure rotates 135° anticlockwise.

Q3 B The three shapes in the top half of the figure move to the bottom half and the two shapes in the bottom half move to the top half. The order and shading of the shapes change. Change the order and shading in the third figure in the same way.

Q4 D The size of the middle shape increases and the other two shapes are removed. The middle shape takes on the colour of the bottom shape and the line style of the top shape.

Q5 C The inner shape rotates 90° and increases in size to become the outer shape. The outer shape rotates 90° clockwise and decreases in size to become the inner shape.

Q6 A Three different-sized versions of the figure are formed. The smallest one has dashed lines, the middle one has dotted lines and the largest one has bold lines.

Q7 B The order of the symbols changes from the order 123456 to 263154.

Q8 D The arrows pointing inside the shape now point in both directions. The arrows pointing outside the shape now point inside.

Q9 C The number of sides of the shape decreases from eight to seven.

Q10 B The large outer shape rotates 135° clockwise and its lines change from solid to dotted.

The small inner shape moves to the other end of the large outer shape and its lines change from dashed to solid.

Test 20

Q1 C In all other figures, the total number of sides of the internal shape(s) equals the number of sides of the large shape.

Q2 B In all other figures, the square is further left than the triangle.

Q3 A All the other figures are rotations of the same shape.

Q4 D In all other figures, the number of circles is greater than the number of clouds.

Q5 D All the other figures consist of a shape and its reflection in a vertical mirror line.

Q6 B In all other figures, the line shading in the circle is in the same direction.

Q7 D In all other figures, the curved line emerges from the right-hand side of the straight line.

Q8 A In all other figures, the black circle is placed in the same position within the trapezium.

Q9 E In all other figures, the same seven symbols each appear once only.

Q10 D In all other figures, from left to right, the arrows rotate in an anticlockwise direction.

Test 21

Q1 E The figure in the top right shows the number of sides of each of the shapes in the figure in the top left.

Therefore, the figure in the bottom right must show the number of sides of each of the shapes in the figure in the bottom left.

Therefore, the answer is E.

Q2 C The figure in the bottom left is formed by rotating the figure in the top left by 90° anticlockwise and by removing the inner circle.

Therefore, these changes must be made to the figure in the top right to form the figure in the bottom right.

Therefore, the answer is C.

Q3 **A** In each row, the middle figure is formed by placing the left and right figures on top of each other and then removing all overlapping lines (if there are any).

Therefore, the answer is A.

Q4 **E** In each row, the shapes rotate 45° clockwise from left to right.

Therefore, the answer is E.

Q5 **E** In each row, the figure contains one more square unit than the previous figure.

Therefore, the missing figure must consist of two square units.

Therefore, the answer is E.

Q6 **D** Each figure in the grid consists of three shapes. The smallest shape has one side fewer than the middle shape, which has one side fewer than the largest shape.

Therefore, the missing figure must follow this rule.

Therefore, the answer is D.

Q7 **B** The figures in each row consist of two halves and a whole.

Therefore, the answer is B.

Q8 **E** The sum of the number of small black circles in each column is 10.

Therefore, the missing figure must consist of six black circles as $10 - 3 - 1 = 6$

Therefore, the answer is E.

Q9 **C** The figure in the top right rearranges the size, colour and rotation of the shapes in the figure in the top left.

Therefore, the same rearrangements must be made to the shapes in the figure in the bottom left to form the figure in the bottom right.

Therefore, the answer is C.

Q10 **A** The figure in the top right is formed by inverting the position and colour of the circles in the figure in the top left. Black circles become white and white circles become black. Circles outside the shape move inside and circles inside the shape move outside.

Therefore, the same changes must be applied to the figure in the bottom left to form the figure in the bottom right.

Therefore, the answer is A.

Test 22

Q1 **B** The figures on the left are each fractions with a value of two.

Therefore, the answer is B.

Q2 **D** In the figures on the left, when the number of dots on the right of the domino are subtracted from the number of dots on the left, the difference is three.

Therefore, the answer is D.

Q3 **A** The figures on the left each show a fraction of the same whole shape that has 12 equal parts.

Therefore, the answer is A.

Q4 **C** The figures on the left each show a larger shape with a smaller version of the same shape inside it. The smaller shape is divided into four equal parts.

Therefore, the answer is C.

Q5 **B** The figures on the left each consist of two shapes. The number of sides of the internal shape is one less than the number of sides of the external shape.

Therefore, the answer is B.

Q6 **E** The figures on the left each consist of a black circle with a number of shapes protruding from it. The number of shapes protruding from each circle equals the number of lines that each shape consists of.

Therefore, the answer is E.

Q7 **C** The figures on the left each consist of a grid containing the same white shape and a black shape diagonally opposite to it.

Therefore, the answer is C.

Q8 **E** The figures on the left each consist of a triangle that contains an even number of black circles.

Therefore, the answer is E.

Q9 **D** The figures on the left each consist of a shape containing two rows of black circles. The bottom row always has two more black circles than the top row.

Therefore, the answer is D.

Q10 **B** The figures on the left are each arrows with one point.

Therefore, the answer is B.

Test 23

Q1 A

Q2 D

Q3 D

Q4 B

Q5 B

Q6 A

Q7 B

Q8 B

Q9 D

Q10 D

Test 24

Q1 B

Q2 C

Q3 D

Q4 C

Q5 C

Q6 B

Q7 B

Q8 C

Q9 D

Q10 A

Test 25

Q1 A

Q2 A

Q3 C

Q4 B

Q5 D

Q6 C

Q7 B

Q8 A

Q9 B

Q10 D

Notes

Notes